ME
&
SNAP

*True tales of two young brothers living,
loving, and laughing their way
through the 40s, 50s, and early 60s
in the Heartland's small town
of Carroll, Iowa*

Cover Design by April A. Adams
www.AdamsAdmin.com

ISBN: 978-0-9821336-4-4

TABLE OF CONTENTS

Me & Snap

INTRODUCTION

My primary reason for recording the events of these youthful years is for the pure and simple enjoyment of my children and grandchildren.

My two incredible daughters (Chrissy and Jenny) and my wonderful wife, Connie, have been lovingly prompting me for years to do this. So, here you have it. Not all of it, but some of it.

Growing up in Carroll, Iowa in the 40s, 50s, and early 60s was so exciting and so much fun that words cannot capture the reality of it all. My brother Snap and I were Mark Twain's *Tom Sawyer* and *Huck Finn* with one major difference. We actually did all this stuff and somehow lived to tell about it.

Each chapter is written according to my recollections. There was no collaboration with Snap or any other characters in this book. Some of the names have been changed to protect the privacy of certain individuals and their families. I have written as if I were telling the story at that age and corresponding state of mind. It's not intended to be perfect prose. Far from it!

It's an effort to take you on a fun-filled journey back to a time and times that should not pass with my passing.

The chapters of this book are not in chronological order. So kick back and read them at any time and in any order that piques your interest.

All of these events truly happened. I know because I was there. And I wrote the book.

I am ... *JOHN WILLIAM BRUNER.*

Chapter 1

SNAP

"Lights Out"

Dateline: Summer, 1957 – Ages 13 & 12

I was born May 22, 1944 and christened John William Bruner. I received John from my grandfather, John Bruner. William was my grandfather Cavanaugh's first name and I have been honored to carry their good names through another generation.

Many people, for various reasons, get tagged with a nickname that sticks for a lifetime. Well, when I was a kid my nickname was "John." When I was a school kid my nickname was "John." When I married my high school sweetheart my nickname was "John." And now getting up in years, my friends and family still call me by my nickname, "John." At first it was hard for me to accept the nickname John, but I've learned to deal with it and when people ask me how I happen to get the nickname "John" I simply tell them, "My brother Snap stuck me with it."

How did he choose the nickname John, they ask? I tell them, "I'm not sure, but he's been calling me that since we were little kids—and it has stuck ever since. He was just a clever little fella!"

Snap was born November 5, 1945, christened Robert Brian Bruner. Robert was our father's name. Brian was someone else's name and Bruner was grandpa's last name. So, where did "Snap" come from?

Well, back in Carroll, Iowa in the '50s, Snap was a young man's man—or something like that. The truth is, I think he discovered hormones before hormones became popular. Anyway, he came by his nickname "Snap" very honestly and with no regrets. I know this to be true because I was there the night he became "Snap." I witnessed it, and as sure as he was the one that stuck me with the nickname "John," I was the one who stuck him with the nickname "Snap."

Sweet Revenge. I LOVE IT.

Oh, the story? Yes, of course. It's important that all the facts be known.

It was a hot summer night in 1957. We were at home in the Boys' Room just kinda pounding on each other for lack of anything better to do when the phone rang. It was for Snap. He asked who it was and Mom said, "Mike."

At that time in our lives no one's voices had changed yet, so the girls sounded like boys and the boys sounded like girls. Nobody could tell the difference and nobody really cared. But this night, Mike was not Mike. Mike was Micki. She just became Mike when Mom answered the phone.

Micki had called to tell Snap that she was home babysitting her younger brothers and was about to put them to bed and was just wondering if he might want to come over and watch television with her. His answer was, "I'll be right over."

Now Micki was the cutest little 12-year-old girl on the planet. What she ever saw in Snap is still one of the world's great mysteries. Anyway, Snap told me where he was going and I asked him, "What for?"

He said, "None of your business."

Big mistake. Big, big mistake.

So when he left the house I called my buddy Cy Farner who just lived across the street. I told him what was going on, so we joined up in his back yard and headed for Micki's house. When we got there, through window-peeking surveillance, we saw them sitting next to each other on the couch. We were really surprised because at that time none of us had held a girl's hand or even thought about kissing one of them.

But now, tonight, all that was going to change. That skinny little 12-year-old brother of mine was going to change the world as we knew it.

Cy and I were not ready for this. We were still kids. Girls were ugly, dumb, loud, stupid, and always trying to be teacher's pet. Really, what were they good for? I guess Snap knew and we didn't. Hate it when that happens.

Well, as Snap was sliding closer and closer to Micki, Cy and I were pushing and shoving each other for a better window position. And darned if we didn't get the

9

church giggles. Oh those church giggles, they got us in more trouble than just in church. But that's another story. Anyway, back to Snap. He heard the laughter, whispered something to Micki, got off the couch, checked the windows and before we knew it ...

ALL THE LIGHTS WENT ...
SNAP!

Chapter 2

Kissin' in the Chicken Coop

"A Magical Moment"

Dateline: Fall, 1960 – Ages 16 & 15

It was a beautiful fall, Friday night. The high school football season was over, so we were free to do whatever we wanted and decided to double date. Snap wasn't old enough for his license yet, so I had the privilege of driving us around in our Mom's 1939, beautiful, light blue Plymouth. You know, that old car had corn stalks sticking out from under it—but that's another story.

Anyway, Snap's girlfriend lived in town and my girlfriend, Connie Schreck, was a country girl who lived seven miles out of town. I asked Snap if he and his date would like to ride with me to pick up Connie and he said, "No, her folks are out for the evening, so I will just stay at her house and when you guys get back to town, pick us up. But don't get in a big hurry."

"Don't get in hurry? Oh, I get it!"

I was driving as fast as that old car could go. I couldn't wait to see Connie. She was so special. I hadn't ever met anyone like her before. We had only been

11

dating a month and she was a senior and I was a junior, but that didn't seem to matter. We just enjoyed hanging out together.

When I arrived, we sat around the living room with her folks and just visited. What wonderful people they were. They made me feel right at home and I loved that. After about a half hour the conversation somehow turned to the brooder house that was currently full of baby chicks—dozens of them! Since I had shared my pigeon stories with them, Connie's mom, Rose, suggested that Connie take me to the brooder house to see all these little creatures. It was a great idea. I was excited to go there and also happy to spend some time alone with Connie.

We entered the brooder house (I always called it the chicken coop). There they were: dozens of cute, tiny, cuddly, baby chicks. Connie invited me to pull up a seat so we both grabbed a five gallon feed bucket, turned it upside-down and settled in for a very special event.

As the chicks swarmed around us, Connie picked one of them up and said, "John, watch this."

She laid the little chick on its back in the palm of her hand and ever so gently rubbed on its tiny little neck and breast. After 10 -15 seconds of this, the little guy rested his head back, closed his eyes, unfolded his wings and went into a deep slumber. Darndest thing I had ever seen. Then I tried it, and to my great surprise, it worked. She did it again and so did I. Within ten minutes, half the chicks in that chicken coop were asleep at our feet. The little chicks would wake up and run back to us and we were just laughing and laughing; loving every moment of it and our time together.

As we picked up the chicks, our hands would occasionally touch and we'd look at each other and smile. Something magical was happening. I turned, and looking into her beautiful, beautiful face and with all the courage I could muster out of my skinny 135-pound body, I asked, almost in a whisper, "Can I kiss you?"

Her eyes gave a brief flutter and she said, "Okay."

At that moment we very cautiously … very tenderly … very lovingly … kissed … in the chicken coop. That was November, 1960.

On September 4, 1965 …

WE WERE MARRIED!

Me & Snap

Chapter 3

The Hunt for Maggie's Gold

"Ambushed at the Plantation"

Dateline: October or November 1954 – Ages 10 & 9

We had some good friends, Harold and Jim, both of whom lived about six blocks from us and very near Maggie's Plantation.

Harold was in Snap's class and Jim in mine. Our two buddies knew the legend of Maggie's Gold and talked about it very often. According to these boys, Maggie lived through the Great Depression and learned not to trust banks or bankers, so she took her considerable wealth and bought solid gold bars. She knew that a lot of people in town had learned of her wealth and the gold bars, so she took them out to her plantation and buried them in places where only she knew they could be found.

Now The Plantation, as we kids called it, was actually 5-10 acres of mostly woods and her big old farm house. Our pals swore that she had hired armed guards to patrol her property to keep the treasure hunters out. Well, that scared us, but we had been scared before.

One day after school in the fall of that year, we were looking for adventure and Snap said, "Let's look for Maggie's Gold."

We all liked the idea, so the four of us loaded our BB guns and headed for The Plantation. Our plan was to find the gold, haul it out of there, be rich and quit school. The quitting school thing was just a joke, but getting rich was definitely our plan.

When we headed out from Harold's house that day, his parents were not home, so we left the front door open—just in case.

The four of us arrived at the plantation ready for anything, but determined to carry out our mission. Side-by-side we marched on to Maggie's golden ground.

After advancing a good twenty yards, all hell broke loose. Gun shots, cannon fire, you name it!

Maggie's Army was advancing against us with reckless abandon. We could have taken cover and returned fire, but instead we did what all battlefield cowards do. We turned around and ran like hell!

You've never seen four skinny little butts run so fast. We ran with Olympic speed. We passed each other, then passed each other again! We blasted through the front door of Harold's house, went into his bedroom and slammed the door. We were scared and knew we had been shot up pretty bad. We stripped our clothes off so we could identify our wounds and bullet holes. But to our great surprise and happiness, there were no wounds. There were no bullet holes! With all that fire power, how could they have missed?

As we began to talk about our cowardly retreat from Maggie's Plantation, Snap told us that he stopped twice, dropped to one knee, and returned fire with his *Daisy Red Ryder*, lever-action BB gun.

That didn't surprise us because everyone in the neighborhood knew that Snap had more guts than anybody else. But, until our defeat at Maggie's Plantation, we didn't realize he was also the fastest kid in the neighborhood! He had to be the fastest. No one else could have stopped twice, fired at the bad guys and still been the first one in our friend's house. To this day, I'm still amazed at his guts and speed.

A few days after our humiliating defeat at the *Battle of Maggie's Plantation,* we learned from Harold's dad that Maggie had gone to the Carroll Police Department to get a permit to have members of the Carroll Gun Club come to her place to shoot noisy, dirty blackbirds.

Isn't it amazing? Here we thought we had encountered a large enemy force that had us out-numbered and out-gunned. But as it turned out, they were not even shooting at us. No wonder we didn't find any bullet holes!

We never did go back to hunt for Maggie's Gold, and it wasn't because we found out the truth—that the gold was in the bank all the time, not in the ground. No, we didn't go back for an entirely different reason. We always talked about how brave and how tough we were, but the truth is, we were …

A COUPLE OF LITTLE COWARDS!

Me & Snap

Chapter 4

Almost Went to HELL

"Bless Me Father, for I Have Sinned"

Dateline: Fall, 1964 – Ages 20 & 19

This chapter may not hold the excitement of many of our more youthful adventures. But believe me, we were a lot more scared and worried than any other time in our lives—because we thought we might go to HELL. It happened while we were students at the University of South Dakota.

To get the full impact of this chapter, it's important that you understand a couple of issues about our Catholic faith as we were taught it by the priests and nuns.

First of all, it was a mortal sin to eat meat on Friday—all Fridays, not just during Lent.

Secondly, if you did eat meat on Friday and died before getting to confession, you went straight down— down to HELL to burn forever and ever. Now how scary is that????

So we never did eat meat on Friday, until this one Friday night in November, 1964. It happened after class.

As usual, we were thirsty so we headed to our favorite watering hole in downtown Vermillion, South Dakota, called *Careys*.

We had a few beers, shot pool, had a few more beers and shot some more pool. While taking a break from shooting pool, we bellied up to the bar and began talking about how hungry we were.

Now remember, it's 1964. We're Catholic. It's Friday, and right in front of us was a box of *Slim Jims*—long sticks of beautiful, fatty, high sodium, spicy, delicious beef sticks. We knew how delicious they were because we ate bunches of them every day except Fridays. We continue to be amazed, after eating all those *Slim Jims*, that we are still alive and telling this story.

Anyway, after looking at those beauties over a couple more beers and much soul searching, we decided to play the odds and have … just one.

Man, it tasted so good, but it made us more thirsty, so we had one more short glass of beer.

Well, that beer caused us to be hungry again so—you guessed it—we committed another mortal sin!

That was enough. Full of beer, full of *Slim Jims* and full of guilt, we walked back to the Phi Delt house to get some sorely needed sleep.

I'm not sure how well Snap slept that night, but I didn't sleep at all. I was afraid of going to sleep and never waking up and going to HELL, forever and ever.

Our favorite young priest friend was hearing confessions the next day at 1:00 p.m. and I was the first one in line. Back in those days, the first thing you said to the priest when you went to confession was, "Bless me Father, for I have sinned."

Father was a great priest and he knew us guys real well, so when I got in the confessional I said, "Bless me Father, for I have sinned. This is John!"

He replied, "Oh, hi John, how are things going?"

I told him, "Okay," but that I slipped last night and committed a mortal sin or two.

He simply replied, "Well, tell me about these mortal sins."

I gave it to him blow-by-blow (or bite-by-bite) and even shared the fact that my dear brother was a co-conspirator in this terrible deed. When I was done, he asked, "Is that it?"

I said, "Yes, Father, and I am heartily sorry for these and all my sins and I ask for God's forgiveness."

He then said, "John, you and Snap didn't commit a mortal sin last night. As a matter of fact, I don't think you committed any sin at all. The Catholic Church wants its members to be disciplined, and that's why it has certain rules. We all break the rules now and then, but that doesn't mean we are bad people, and that doesn't mean we are going to HELL. Now listen, you and Snap are good guys and for your penance, say one Hail Mary; and please say it for me."

As I left the confessional full of great peace and joy, I shared a smile with the next person in line. And as

I walked a few steps further, I faintly heard that person say, "Bless me Father, for I have sinned…

"THIS IS SNAP!"

Chapter 5

Pigeon Pie & Pigeon Poop

"Just Little Guys"

Dateline: 1954 – Ages 10 & 9

When we were just little guys, a nice girl by the name of Lorraine Wiederin lived with us during the week to help Mom. It was wild around our house, and Mom needed all the help she could get. Lorraine lived on a farm five miles north of Carroll. Every Saturday, the folks gave her a ride home and Snap and I would always ride along.

One Saturday she asked if we would like to spend the rest of the weekend on the farm with her mom, dad, brother Ralph, and herself. We begged Mom and Dad to let us stay. They didn't hesitate a bit to say yes (surprise, surprise). They needed frequent breaks from us two little guys.

What a weekend; it was a blast! We rode their plow horses, caught real live, beautiful pigeons, peed and pooped in a real outhouse, got to touch a real electric fence, wrestled Mr. Wiederin, ate pigeon pie, slept in a down-filled feather bed, and on Sunday, went to Mass at a real country church in Mount Carmel. It was a fantastic experience. We had become country boys; and we loved it!

After that, we spent every weekend we could on the farm. The Wiederins were such wonderful people, who seemed genuinely happy to have us stay with them. We even rode our bikes out there on some Saturdays, spent the day and rode back home in the late afternoon. It was a hard five mile ride on gravel roads and we were little guys who got hot, tired and stinky. But we didn't care!

Snap and I were fascinated with pigeons. We caught them in the barn and Mrs. Wiederin would clean and cook them for us. And sometimes we'd bring them home and Mom would cook them. Man, oh man, were they ever good! Pigeon stew. Pigeon pie. Pigeon cooked any way was our favorite food.

After several months of catching and eating these beautiful birds, we decided to raise them. Mom and Dad were not too happy about this, but gave us permission to raise "a few." We went down to the Fareway Grocery store and the nice manager, Mr. Singsang, gave us some large wooden fruit crates. We put some chicken wire over the front of them, and bingo—we had our pigeon houses!

Dad took us out to the Wiederin farm a couple of nights so Lorraine and Ralph could help us catch just the ones we wanted. It was easy to catch them. Just point the flashlight at them in the barn. They would freeze or fly into the wall. We grabbed them, bagged them and took them to their new home. We wanted only the most beautiful of the pigeons—the white ones and the brown ones.

We had a dozen pigeons. We loved them and they grew to love us, too. We gave them all names. The prettiest white pair we named *King* and *Queen*. We had caught one of their little white babies, also. She was a beauty and we named her *Junior*.

The most striking pair we had was brown and white. The male we named *Cong*, and the female, *Lady*. They really loved each other; they were always side-by-side with their wings touching.

We really, really loved our pigeons. We would run home after school, open their cages and they would fly out and sit on the roof of the house for a few minutes. Then they would fly down and sit on our shoulders, heads, or hands—any place they could find to sit on us. And even though we knew they were lovin' us up, in their excitement, they would poop on us. And, we didn't even care! They were our pets. They were our friends. And I'll say it again—we really loved them.

However, a problem soon developed. Our pigeons flew around after school until it got dark, then flew back into their cages. Before we went to bed each night, we went out to close and lock the cage doors so no predators could get them. But we began to notice there were more than just our white and brown ones in our pigeon houses. There were blue ones. Lots and lots of blue pigeons!

At first, we thought it was pretty cool, until our "beautiful dozen" grew to ten dozen and they were flying around the neighborhood pooping on everyone's roof!

Dad was a lawyer at the time, and the County Attorney. One night after work, he told us the neighbors were complaining to the police, so we had to get rid of the pigeons. That night we went into the cages and sacked them all up. All of them. White ones. Brown ones. Blue ones. There must have been 90 to 100 pigeons, and we took them all back to the farm.

The next morning, they were all back sitting on our roof and the neighbors' roofs doing what pigeons do best.

Snap and I knew instinctively that something terrible was going to happen. Dad said we had to get our BB guns and shoot them!

No way! We couldn't do that. We loved them. So, Dad got some high school boys who lived in the neighborhood to shoot and kill all of them. They put them in large potato sacks and threw them into garbage cans—all of them except our "beautiful dozen."

As they tumbled to the ground, mortally wounded, we cradled them in our hands and arms to carry them ever so lovingly to their final resting place— our backyard. There we dug a shallow grave, laid them beside their respective partners (with *Cong* and *Lady* pressed tightly together, wing-to-wing, for eternity) covered them with God's warm earth and a couple of Mom's flowers, and stood there. We didn't say any prayers **because we were just little guys**. We didn't tell each other how sad we were, **because we were just little guys**. We just stood there, side-by-side, hung our heads and cried. Because ...

WE WERE JUST LITTLE GUYS!

Me & Snap

Chapter 6

Forts in the Jungle

"Pukin' from the Tree Tops"

Dateline: 1950 through 1955 – Ages 5 to 10

The "Jungle" started about one hundred yards east of our house, running north and south for about three city blocks. There was a wide open area in the middle of the Jungle about the size of a football field, and the rest of it was, well, Jungle. There were trees and more trees. We climbed all of them and fell out of most of them.

The Jungle was one of our favorite playgrounds. We spent many a day there, and even some nights. We played ball there, chased wild critters there, knocked monkeys out of trees there (Snap, our friends and I were the monkeys), and built forts there. Our forts were a thing of beauty. They were huge piano boxes that we purchased from Mr. Wagner, who just lived up the street from us. He sold pianos for a living. Five bucks a box and we were the proud owners of two of them. No mortgage; we owned them free and clear.

Our fort was two stories high. We stacked one box on top of the other. The first floor was where we

29

stored our food, BB guns, comic books and toilet paper.
Yes, we did a lot of poopin' and peein' in the Jungle, so
we needed that stuff. The fort's second floor was our war
room and bedroom. We painted pictures on the walls
and laid some old carpet on the floor. It was the neatest
fort on the planet.

Our neighborhood of kids was about ten square
blocks and there were dozens of kids our age and a bunch
of kids a few years older. We were all mostly friends, but
for the sake of "war games," we formed gangs. The
Bruner Gang, the *Farner Gang*, the *Moen Gang*, the *Stoffers
Gang*, the *Wilson Gang*, and a few other gangs from outside
our turf. Most of the time, the *Farner Gang* and the *Bruner
Gang* were allies. As a matter of fact, Cy Farner helped us
buy, build and defend our fort. He was our good buddy;
we could always depend on Cy.

When the gangs got together, we wrestled, boxed
(each of us had a pair of boxing gloves), had pea-shooter
fights, slingshot battles (these were dangerous), and tree-
climbing challenges (two guys climbed the same tree; then
kicked, pushed, slugged and stomped on each other's feet
and hands until one guy was knocked out of the tree).

Occasionally, some bad blood developed and
threats were exchanged. One such threat came from an
opposing gang member who Snap knocked out of the
tree. He told us he would be back and destroy our fort.
We made it very clear to him that it would be the biggest
mistake of his young life.

A week after this incident, the Bruner and Farner
families took off for their annual summer vacation to
Lake Okoboji. The two families were very close, and for

many years, vacationed together. However, before we left, Snap, Cy and I went to the Jungle to add a little extra protection to our fort. We dug a three-foot tiger trap right in front of the ground floor entrance. We collected some dog dung, dropped it in the bottom of the trap, then covered the trap with sticks and grass. If anyone tried anything while we were gone, they would pay dearly for their aggression!

We had a great vacation, and as soon as we got back, we ran out into the Jungle to check on our fort. We came upon our worst nightmare—our fort was destroyed! As a matter of fact, it was torched—burned to the ground! Our blood was boiling, but we knew one thing for certain; one of those guys got swallowed up by our tiger trap. It was caved in and the stuff on the bottom was flattened against the ground, and did it ever stink!

Remember, we warned those guys what would happen if they attacked our fort. So Snap, Cy and I grabbed our Cub Scout hatchets and a handful of cherry bombs and headed up the jungle trail to destroy the enemy's fort. Their fort was a beauty, just like ours—two stories and sturdy. When we arrived, no one was there.

We quickly went about our business. Snap and I worked on the side walls, and Cy climbed up on the roof and jumped up and down until it caved in. We were doing this during broad daylight, so we needed to finish it and get out of there. We packed our gear, lobbed a few cherry bombs into what was left of the fort, and retreated to the safety of our turf. Wow, we really did a job on that fort! The cherry bombs started it on fire and we could see it burning two blocks away.

That evening the phone rang and Dad spent about ten minutes talking to someone. When he got off he said, "Boys, up to your room; we need to have a talk."

I hated it when he said that!

As it turned out, the person on the phone was the grandma of the boy whose fort we destroyed. She was in the kitchen at the time of our raid and she watched the entire event. Dad asked, "Did you do it?"

"Yes, but he destroyed our fort first."

Dad told us that the other boy told his folks he *didn't* destroy our fort.

We said, "Dad, you are a lawyer; let's have a trial, because he's a liar!"

Well, as it turned out we had to buy that liar two new piano boxes. That was a bad deal and now we were broke. We walked back into the Jungle and tried to let go of some of our anger and disappointment when, out of the blue, Snap said, "John, I have a great idea, let's build our new fort there."

He was pointing to the biggest tree in the jungle. Yes, a fort in the tree. It was a great idea—Snap was a smart guy!

There were a lot of new houses being built in our neighborhood, so we decided to borrow some of their lumber. When the builders left at the end of the day, we would pick up the discarded nails and wood and haul it over to our tree. We built a great tree fort in the Jungle with a window to the north, a window to the south, and a trap door on the floor so we could get in and out of the fort. We accidentally built the fort at a slant, so it was hard to stand up in it. We loved it anyway and supplied it with crackers, comic books, our *Daisy Red Ryder* BB guns, toilet paper, sling shots, a bucket of rocks, a bucket of water, a bucket of sand and, just for good measure, a couple of Swisher Sweet cigars. I won't tell you how we got those cigars, but when we tried to smoke them, we got so sick we were both hanging out the windows, "pukin' from the tree tops." Talk about sick!

Oh, the buckets. The rocks were for our slingshots, the water was dumped on invaders trying to climb up to our fort, and the bucket of sand followed the water. When those guys were wet, the sand really stuck to them! After we soaked and sanded them, you should have heard them swear at us. Their favorite description of us was, "You little sonsab _ _ _ _ es!"

They gave us the finger while firing their slingshots and BB guns into the windows of our fort. Those guys couldn't take a joke!

One time when Snap and I were in our tree fort, four guys a couple of years older than us approached our fort, spoiling for a fight (surprise, surprise). We asked them what they wanted and their response was, "We want you two little chicken sh _ _ s to come down and fight."

Chicken sh _ _ s? That was a pretty cool swear word! We liked it, so we challenged them back with their own words, "Come up and get us, you chicken sh _ _s!"

AND THE BATTLE WAS ON!

Me & Snap

Chapter 7

Pooped My Pants

"Buried in the Jungle"

Dateline: 1953 – Ages 9 & 8

One late afternoon in the early fall of 1953, Snap, CY and I were in the Jungle just kinda hanging out and looking for a little action. We knew that someone was building a big new house on the northeast corner of "our" Jungle, so we decided to scout it out. When we got there, we huddled behind a huge pile of dirt about 30 feet from the new structure. The walls were up. The roof was on. And the contractor and owners of the house were in there, walking around and talking about stuff we really didn't understand.

You know by now that we were little guys who imagined ourselves as warriors, cowboys, supermen and soldiers. So at this particular time, one of us suggested that we lob some hand grenades on the roof of this new house to disrupt all the fun they seemed to be having.

All three of us thought that was a great idea, so we all grabbed a big dirt clod, kept our elbows locked, (as WWII army guys did) and launched our dirt clod hand grenades onto the roof.

35

BOOM, BOOM, BOOM!

All three were direct hits on the roof—right above where they were standing. We heard them shout, "What in the heck was that?"

One of the men said, "I think I know."

This was way too much fun. Those people didn't have a clue. I said to Snap and CY, "Reload!"

We each grabbed another hand grenade, locked our elbows, and launched. Direct hits—BOOM, BOOM, BOOM!

Didn't get much more fun than that—until all of a sudden out of nowhere—this humongous adult man jumps out at us and screams, "What the hell are you kids doing?"

Total shock. My entire mind, body and soul were devastated. Nothing like this had ever happened to me before. When he appeared out of nowhere and hollered, "What the hell are you kids doing?" I POOPED MY PANTS!

God's truth. I couldn't believe it. I was on my knees when it happened and I had no idea what to do. I froze. This man kept hollering at us and telling us we were good kids, so he couldn't understand why we were behaving like this. He went on and on.

I was so unprepared for all of this, I just started nervously laughing. I couldn't stop. Snap and Cy started laughing, and the more we laughed, the angrier our new neighbor got. Finally, after chewing our butts out for a good ten minutes, he said, "Now get the hell out of here before I really get mad!"

Heck, we had the impression he already was really mad, but we did as he ordered and retreated deep into the Jungle. When we got there, I told Snap and Cy that this guy's sudden appearance and loud hollering shocked my system so severely that, "I pooped my pants!"

Oh man, did they laugh! And that was okay, but when they finally got over it, I made them promise they would never, never, ever tell anyone that I pooped my pants. They said they would never tell. They were my best friends, and I knew I could trust them.

A couple of problems still remained. I needed some clean jeans and skivvies. I asked Snap to sneak in the house and round up some clean clothes for me. While he was gone, I went into our Jungle fort, took off my soiled clothes, and used the toilet paper there to clean up as best I could. In a few minutes, Snap was back. I put on the clean skivs and jeans. Then we discussed the one final problem. What should we do with the dirty clothes?

I couldn't tell Mom and Dad that I pooped my pants. I was nine years old. **Nine-year-olds don't poop their pants!** If I did admit to pooping my pants, they would start asking a bunch of questions. I didn't want to tell them that we had launched an unprovoked attack against our new neighbors in their new house, and when he counter attacked I ... well—lost it!

There was only one thing we could do—get rid of the evidence. Hide 'em. Burn 'em. Bury 'em. Bury 'em in the Jungle. Once again, Snap was called upon to go home undetected, get Dad's spade and return to the Jungle.

He did a great job. We dug a two-foot hole, buried the evidence and got home just in time for supper. Only one problem. Dad and Mom saw us put the spade back in the garage.

Well, we sat down for supper, prayed and filled our plates; then, the dreaded conversation began.

Mom very pointedly asked, "Boys, what were you doing with the spade? Snap, I saw you carrying it, so what did you guys use it for? Now tell me the truth, I don't want any more of your buried treasure or other funny stories."

"Okay, Mom. We were playing in the Jungle. John accidentally pooped his pants. He didn't want you to know, so we buried his jeans in the Jungle."

Snap always had a way of making Mom and Dad laugh, so when he told them this, they cracked up.

When they composed themselves, Mom said…

"VERY FUNNY, SNAP. NOW, WHAT REALLY HAPPENED?"

Chapter 8

Golfing Black Birds

"What's So Funny?"

Dateline: 1954 – Ages 10 & 9

One day in June or July of 1954, Mom called Snap and me into the kitchen and said, "Boys, those black birds are eating so many of those cherries in our tree, I don't think there will be any left for me to make pies or jam. I'm just sick about it. I need you two to help me keep those birds out of our cherry tree."

Snap asked, "Do you want us to shoot 'em?"

"Oh, I don't know, but you have got to help me."

I said, "Mom, the only way to get them out of there is to shoot 'em!"

"Okay, do what you have to, but don't tell your dad I gave you permission to shoot them with your BB guns. Promise?"

"We promise. But Mom, when we shoot them, what do you want us to do with them?"

She responded, "What did you do with all the other birds you've shot? I haven't seen any of them lying around the neighborhood, and I know you are shooting them because we don't hear birds singing around here in the morning."

That was a cheap shot (pardon the pun)! Every kid on the block had a BB gun. We didn't shoot all those early morning song birds. Heck, we were still sleeping when those birds started to make all that racket.

Anyway, we devised a plan. One of us would climb the tree with our BB gun, shoot those thievin' black birds, and the other guy would get rid of them.

You know, we were not very smart. We reasoned to ourselves that if they were not in our yard—no problem. So, we decided that the guy below the tree would simply put them in someone else's yard. But how would we do that?

Snap—genius that he was—came up with the perfect solution. "Let's use Uncle Cliff's golf club and just knock them over the hedge into Mr. Maher's backyard."

Perfect! I climbed the tree and Snap was on the ground with a vintage nine-iron from the 20's. The birds were all over the place, gobbling up Mom's pie and jam. I took careful aim and began dropping them on top of Snap. He carefully measured them, and then launched them over a five-foot high hedge into Mr. Maher's backyard. It wasn't necessarily a work of art, but it was working. We were just about to celebrate our victory over these berry-eating invaders when, from around the hedge, appeared Mr. Maher holding two or three birds in each hand. I jumped out of the tree and he stomped up to within five feet of us asking, "Are these your birds?"

Let me tell you, Mr. Maher was a good man and we liked him, but at this moment we were scared spitless—or something like that. Snap, never one to tell a lie when caught in the act, answered, "Yes."

Then Mr. Maher said, "If these are your birds, what the **HELL** are they doing in **my** backyard?"

I told him the story about cherry pies and jam and that Mom told us to get rid of the black birds. He stood there holding those birds and said, "Let me get this straight. These birds were eating all the cherries in this big tree, so your mom told you to shoot them. Is that right?"

"Yes sir," replied our spokesman, Snap.

"So, John climbed the tree and shot them?"

"Yes, sir."

"So when they fell to the ground, Snap threw them in my backyard?"

"No, sir."

"Then how the **HELL** did they get in my backyard?"

"I golfed them over there, Mr. Maher."

"You golfed them into my backyard?"

"Yes, sir, but from now on I'm going to golf them into the Jungle."

Mr. Maher pointed to the Jungle, then held the birds up a little higher, looked right at both of us and said, "You two are the most unbelievable little sh _ _ s that God ever created!"

41

Then he dropped the birds, turned, and walked away. We noticed as he walked toward his house that his shoulders were shaking. We knew that meant he was either laughing or crying. We sure hoped he wasn't crying; and, if he was laughing...

WE COULDN'T FIGURE OUT WHAT WAS SO FUNNY!

Chapter 9

Snap's on Fire

"Farts with Flames"

Dateline: Christmas Eve, 1958 – Ages 14 & 13

When we were growing up, our fun time and play time repertoire was full of wrestling, boxing, fishing, basketball, football, telling the truth, telling lies, climbing trees, falling out of trees, playing on roof tops, falling off roof tops, riding horses, getting bucked off horses, camping, trapping, making kites, flying kites, cops and robbers, strip poker, pool, tents, cigars, forts, and … *farts*!

Okay, we weren't vulgar little boys; we were just normal little guys. We learned stuff. We tried stuff. One day we added "lighting farts" to our list of daily activities.

Our good buddy Cy Farner told us about it.

We told him we didn't believe it, so he got down on his back on his kitchen floor (no one was home), waited a few minutes, struck a match, held it down by the seat of his pants, and …

BANG!

Lighting shot out of his butt.

COOL!! It was easy, harmless, and it was fun!

We learned this when we were about eight or nine and engaged in this activity with great regularity. We were couth little guys and always did this privately, very seldom bragging about the exceptionally "good ones."

However, there was one that topped them all. It was Christmas Eve, 1958. Mom served her traditional, wonderful oyster stew, chili, pies and candy—you name it, Mom had it there for us. There was no better mom, or cook, in the whole world, and we ate it all. We opened presents, laughed, talked and teased until about 11:00, then Dad announced it was time for bed. Santa was on his way and we were going to 8:00 Mass in the morning. While we were helping pick up, Snap accidentally passed gas. Oh, it was ripe—really ripe—and I dared him to light "one of those things." Our younger brother, Barry, who was six at the time, told us to quit talking dirty. I told him, "Farts are natural gas and you really can light them!"

He said, "Liar."

We told him to stick around and watch.

Dad, Mom (who was pregnant with brother Dave), and sisters, Judy and Mary Fran, headed upstairs to bed. Snap and I told them we wanted to show Toad something and we'd be right up. (Toad was little brother Barry's nickname.)

Our Uncle Stan and Aunt Gertrude gave us the same present every Christmas—fuzzy cotton pajamas, which we were wearing. We were in the living room. I turned the lights off, Snap laid down on his back (remember we only did this with pants on), struck a match, expelled one of those nasty things, and:

"KABOOM!"

I've never seen such bright, brilliant colors in my whole life! And, it's the first and last time I have ever seen a human being totally engulfed in flames. The combination of fuzzy pajamas and that gas explosion had old Snap torched from top to toes.

Barry screamed and ran upstairs. Snap sprang to his feet and I was whacking him with a throw rug. The burn time was probably five to six seconds. He wasn't hurt a bit, but those pajamas sure looked and smelled awful! Snap about burned up on that Christmas Eve, but we couldn't stop laughing.

As a matter of fact, that was fifty years ago…

AND WE ARE STILL LAUGHING!

Me & Snap

Chapter 10

Custer Rides Again!

"Who's Custer?"

Dateline: 1964 – Ages 20 & 19

It was a cold November Friday and we were finished with our classes at USD for the week. Five of us fraternity brothers decided it would be fun to head up to Yankton (about 40 miles away), and go to the popular Yankton College bar named *Tommy T's*. Before leaving, we stopped at one of our favorite watering holes, *The Varsity*, and had a few cold ones.

We piled into one of the guys' 1957 Chevy and headed for what would turn out to be one of the wildest, craziest, and most dangerous evenings of our lives. You see, the Yankton college guys didn't particularly like the USD guys, and the USD guys didn't particularly like the Yankton College guys. Believe it or not, we were not looking for trouble. We were only looking for a little excitement, and brother, did we find it!

Just a few miles out of Yankton, it became pretty obvious to Snap and me that one of the guys with us, Ted Simpson, had spent more time at *The Varsity* then the rest of us. We made it real clear to him not to start any trouble. He said, "Don't worry boys. We'll just have a good time."

Ted Simpson was a tall handsome dude and a very good friend of ours. But after a few beers, he would always stir up a little trouble that, most of the time, resulted in a verbal exchange, but sometimes a few punches were thrown. Well—you guessed it—Snap and I were heading for the wrong place, at the wrong time, with the wrong guy.

When we walked into *Tommy T's*, we were greeted by this 230-pound, skinhead bouncer who checked our IDs. He gave us a little smile and said, "Don't drink too much!"

That was good advice, but it came too late for Simpson. From the moment we set foot in that bar, Ted just looked around and thought he was Custer.

Who was Custer? He was a famous Civil War general from the North. After the war, he was sent out west to put down the Indian uprisings. Custer thought he was invincible. No one could defeat him. Well, one fateful day in 1876, Custer and 250 men of the United States 7th Cavalry lined up and charged headlong into 5,000 very angry Sioux Indians at the Little Big Horn River in southeastern Montana. That was *Custer's Last Stand*.

So, here we are in *Tommy T's*, four nice guys and Custer. We sat down in a booth right next to the dance floor. The place was packed and the dance floor was rockin' with Yankton college kids. We ordered a pitcher of beer and five glasses, which we quickly filled. But before we could even take a drink, Simpson just smiled at us, then launched his full glass of beer, (including the glass) over his shoulder onto the dance floor!

Snap shouted at him, "Good God Simpson, what the hell have you done?"

With that, Simpson grabbed my full glass and did it again! You should have heard the swearing and screaming on the dance floor. There were "5,000 very angry Sioux warriors out there wanting to kill Custer."

The other two guys with us did the smart thing. After Simpson threw the first glass, they bolted out the door and ran for the car.

We knew what was going to happen, and it did. A bunch of guys rushed our booth and said, "Which one of you sonsa _ _ _ _ _ es threw the beer on us?"

Simpson just smiled and raised his hand. They jerked him out of the booth and *Custer's Last Stand* was happening for the **second** last time!

We had to make a decision—run or fight. Well, we always thought of ourselves as a couple of rough ridin', fightin' Yankee boys, so with a quick and determined brotherly glance, we decided to **ride into hell with Custer**. So, with no regrets—we joined the battle.

As we were sliding out of the booth—locked and loaded—we kept hollering at each other, "Stay together! Stay together! Stay together!"

We always tried to protect each other from the time we were little guys. As we exited the booth, sure enough, there were two fine young fellas waiting there for us with fists cocked. They only had one major problem—they were way, way too slow. We unloaded a couple of straight right hands before they could pull the trigger. And, that was the end of that battle for our two Yankton college friends.

All of a sudden we found ourselves in the middle of the darndest bar room brawl you could ever imagine. There were 50 to 60 people kickin', screamin', fightin', bitin', pushin', swearin' and throwin' beer all over the place. Now, that might sound bad, and it was; but it was good for Snap and me because they weren't all fighting us. They were fighting anybody in front of them.

Snap and I did get separated. I don't know how many times I slipped on that beer-soaked dance floor. It had to be three or four times. And, every time I tried to get up, someone either fell over me, slugged me, or stepped on me—and that included some of those college girls. Who taught them how to fight? No matter; it was absolute, total chaos. I finally got up and began looking for Snap. I found him over by the booth that we had been sitting in at the time Simpson incited the entire Sioux Nation. And there he was, on the floor. He had some big, bald guy in a headlock. I recognized that bald head, it wasn't just any bald-headed guy—it was the "bouncer!" Snap was fighting the bouncer! Of all the guys that were fighting out there on the floor, Snap had to pick the biggest, meanest dude on the planet. Unbelievable!

Just as I was about to tag-team with Snap, some dirty little coward slugged him in the back of the head. I immediately shot my right fist into the middle of that little coward's face and dropped him like a bad habit.

Ouch! I injured my right hand with that shot, and the next thing I knew I was rolling across the dance floor and banged up against the far wall. As I pulled myself up to a sitting position—trying to clear the cobwebs—two more guys came charging at me. I didn't have much fight left in me, so I just put both arms in front of my face and prepared to take a beatin'. It didn't happen. They instead knelt down beside me and asked if I was okay. I told them, "I think so!"

They then helped me up and told me to get out of there, warning, "The cops are coming!"

Holy cow, the cops were coming! Everyone in *Tommy T's* was heading for the door. Where was Snap? I wasn't leaving without him. There he was, standing by the bar pushing and shoving with—you guessed it—the bouncer!

I wedged myself between the two of them and said, "Snap, we've gotta go; the cop's are coming."

The sirens were getting louder. Snap said he wanted to "finish it" with the bouncer, and I said, "We'll come back later. Let's go!"

I leaned a shoulder into him and pushed him out the door. The street was full of college kids running every which way, and there in the street, lay Simpson, all beat up and smiling. Across the street, in the car, were our two non-combative Phi Delt brothers. Snap and I scooped Simpson off the street and pushed him into the backseat. Just as we were driving away, three black and white police cars and a rather large paddy wagon pulled up in front of *Tommy T's*. How close was that?

As we were leaving Yankton, Simpson asked a stupid question, "Did we win?" Snap fired back, "You idiot Simpson! Did Custer win at the Little Big Horn?"

Simpson hesitated for a moment, then with this great big smile on his bloody face he asked ...

"WHO THE HELL'S CUSTER?"

Chapter 11

Where's Mom Going?

"CRAZY"

Dateline: 1952 – Ages 8 & 7

It was late summer and we were in the back yard shooting hoops. Our favorite uncle, Cliffy, showed up and asked, "What are you two little sh _ _ s doing?"

He always called us that name but we didn't care because other adults called us that, too. So we just always knew they were talking to us when they said, "Hey, you two little sh_ _s."

Anyway, Cliffy had some serious business on his mind. He told us that we were driving Mom crazy and if we didn't "shape up" we were going to *Boys Town*.

Boys Town? "What is Boys Town?" we asked him.

He said it was a place where boys went if they were bad. Snap asked, "How bad do you have to be to go there?"

Cliffy said, "As bad as you two are."

I asked him where Boys Town was and he said, "Omaha."

I asked if that was in Carroll and he said, "Hell no, it's a hundred miles away."

Snap asked him if we were sent there if we had to stay overnight. We couldn't figure out what was so funny, but Cliffy started laughing really hard. When he stopped laughing he said, "You will be there ten thousand nights."

Well, he started laughing again when Snap asked him if ten thousand nights was as many as a hundred nights.

We couldn't figure out all those numbers that Cliffy was talking about, but it seemed longer than a week and we didn't want to be gone that long. Cliffy reached into his pocket and pulled out two one-dollar bills and said, "Listen, you two have got the 'divil' in you, but if you promise to be good boys and be nice to your mom, I'll give you these. But, you've got to promise."

Hey, it's 1952. A dollar can buy almost anything, even, "a promise to be good." So, we promised!

A couple days later, we were ramming around the house and accidentally broke some stuff. I think it was some special plate that Mom loved and a lamp in the family room. As a matter of fact, they were both on the same table that we "accidentally" knocked over when we were wrestling.

We could tell that Mom was both sad and mad at the same time. She said, "Stand right there. Now look at me. I've had it up to here (reaching above her head) with

54

you two. You are driving me crazy! If you don't start being good boys, either you will have to go somewhere or I will have to go somewhere. Now go on, go outside and do whatever you want to do!"

Wow, we really screwed up! Mom was crying. We went next door to Mr. Wagner's house and climbed up on the roof of the south side of his garage. We used to go there a lot because no one could see us there. It was our secret hiding place. We sat down and tried to figure out what Mom just said. We both agreed that we knew where we were going if we continued to be bad— Boys Town!

But where was Mom going? Would she go somewhere with Dad? Would she go to the neighbors'? Would she go to Uncle Cliff's house? Would she go to Grandma's house in Pocahontas?

That's where she was going, because Grandma was her mom. So, that's what she was saying, "You boys are going to Boys Town or I'm going to Grandma's house."

We got it figured out and we didn't like it. We decided we were going to be good boys. We went in the house and found Mom in the kitchen. She looked tired and sad, but we said to her, "Mom, we are going to be good boys forever and ever."

She looked at us and said, "Why are you going to be good boys forever and ever?"

"Because we don't want to go to Boys Town and we don't want you to go to Grandma's. We want you to live with us."

When we said that, her cheeks turned red and her eyes filled up with rain. Then she said, "When I told you that if you don't start being good boys either you will have to go somewhere or I will have to go somewhere, did you think I would send you to Boys Town? Or that I would leave you and move in with Grandma? Is that what you thought?"

We didn't say anything, we just nodded our heads.

Well, we did it again. We made Mom cry. But this time, she wasn't mad at us. We knew she wasn't mad at us, because this time when she was crying ...

SHE WAS HUGGING US.

Chapter 12

Stuck in the Sewer

"RATS"

Dateline: Late Summer 1952 – Ages 8 & 7

It was a hot, early September day and we had just had a great thunderstorm that dropped a whole bunch of rain on Carroll. Whenever that happened, our street flooded and we were out there as soon as the lightning stopped. We would get on our bikes and take about a block run at the flood and see how far we could go before being pulverized by the sheer depth of the water.

On this particular day, we became curious about where the water was disappearing to. As it got lower and lower, we saw the big mouth of the storm sewer swallowing our fun-time flood waters. When the water was all gone, we moved in for a closer look. We got down on our knees, looked down into the sewer, and got very interested in it. It had great "Fort" potential.

The next day after school, we made a quick apple raid and headed for the sewer.

"Apple raid?"

Well, almost every house in Carroll had some kind of fruit tree, so when things ripened, we would grab our salt-shakers (we all had our own shakers) and go shopping for the juiciest fruit in the neighborhood. Most of the neighbors didn't care if we picked an apple or two, but on a couple of occasions, when we started throwing apples at each other and accidentally hit their house, they would holler at us, "Get the hell out of here you little sh_ _s."

Lots of the older people in the neighborhood used to call us that. Anyway, on this day, Snap, Cy Farner and I decided to see if we were skinny enough to squeeze down into that sewer. It had a big, horizontal mouth on it and—guess what?—we slipped right down like sliced bread into a toaster! It was nice down there—kinda dark—but what a great fort! No one could see or find us down there if we were hiding. Perfect. It was our "fox hole fort" and the war games could begin.

We went down there quite a bit and always took our fruit and BB guns with us because, in a real war, the army guys always had their guns and food in the fox holes. We would tell secrets down there, shoot at some of the rats that would occasionally visit, and shoot at birds and squirrels on the other side of the street.

One day as we were walking to our fox hole, a lady from across the street came over and told us someone had shot out one of her windows with what appeared to be a BB gun. She rather tersely asked, "Did you boys do it?"

We told her that we don't shoot our BB guns around houses.

She said, "Well, you have your BB guns with you now and there are nothing but houses all around. So, where are you going to shoot those guns today?"

Snap came up with the perfect answer. "See that sewer? There are rats down there and we are going down there to shoot them."

The nice neighbor lady didn't say any more. She just gave us another one of those funny looks, shook her head, and walked away. That was good, because most of the grownups that got mad at us would say, "We're calling your mom and dad!"

I don't know; we didn't think we were bad kids, but it sure seemed like a lot of older people thought we were!

One late afternoon, when Snap and I were down in our fox hole, one of the neighbor girls, Suzie O'Brien, peeked in and asked what we were doing. We told her, "Playing war."

She asked if she could come down and we said, "Okay, but there's rats down here."

She didn't care. Back in those days, most of the girls that we knew weren't afraid of rats and mice and snakes. Now, Suzie was about our age, but a little thicker than we were. She pushed herself, feet first, down the mouth of the sewer. For a moment she appeared stuck, so we grabbed her ankles, gave a tug and—**plop!** —down she came. She looked around for a little bit and said, "I don't like it down here, I'm getting out."

As it turned out, it was a lot easier said than done. Suzie started crawling out, but got stuck. She was half out and half in. She was stuck tight and pleaded with us, "Please help me! Please!"

Snap crawled out and grabbed her arms; I stayed down and grabbed her feet. Snap pulled; I pushed; Suzie **CRIED**! No luck; still stuck—we tried again. Snap pulled; I pushed; Suzie **SCREAMED**! No luck; still stuck—Snap and I traded places. I pulled; Snap pushed; Suzie about **PASSED OUT**!! No luck; still stuck.

What were we going to do? Suzie was, "Stuck in the Sewer!"

We decided I should run to Suzie's house to get help. She only lived half a block away. Just as I was about to leave, Mom was standing on the front porch hollering, "Boys, come home; it's supper time!"

I hollered back, "We'll be there in a little bit!"

I knocked on the door of Suzie's house. Her mom came to the door and I told her, "Mrs. O'Brien, we need your help. Suzie is stuck in the sewer."

She exclaimed, "Oh, my God!" Then she ran right beside me all the way to the sewer. When Suzie saw her mom, she **really** started crying! Mrs. O'Brien got down on her knees, grabbed Suzie's wrists, and told her she was going to pull her out.

Snap was still down in the sewer and said, "We tried that and it doesn't work."

Mrs. O'Brien looked down into the sewer at Snap and said, *"Shuuuut up!"*

For some reason, Mrs. O'Brien didn't particularly like us that day, but it was okay because back then most adults didn't like kids very much. We understood and it was okay, because we knew some day we would be adults and we probably wouldn't like little kids either. Anyway, Mrs. O'Brien gave a big pull, and . . . **POP!**

Out she came.

Suzie's stomach was scratched up a little bit but, not bad. Mrs. O'Brien looked at us and said, "Do your folks know you two go down there?"

"No."

"Well, you tell them tonight, or I will. Do you understand?"

"Yes, Mrs. O'Brien."

We ran home, sat down at the supper table, and really didn't want to talk. We were hungry and kept our faces to our plates. Then, Mom asked the dreaded question. When we were being interrogated, we took turns answering every other question and, from my recollection, this is pretty much what was said.

"Where were you boys when I called you for supper?"

"We were in our fox hole."

"In your fox hole?"

"Yup."

"Where is your fox hole?"

"In the sewer in front of Moen's house."

"Oh, Good Lord! You boys don't go down in the sewer, do you?"

"Yup."

"Bob (our dad), are you listening to this?"

For some reason, Dad wasn't making eye contact with Mom, but he nodded his head yes.

"What in the world do you boys do down in that stinky old sewer?"

"Tell stories. Eat apples. Shoot rats. Play war."

"You tell stories, eat apples, shoot rats, and play war?"

"Yup."

"What kind of stories do you tell?"

"Secret ones."

"Okay. And the apples—where do you get them?"

"The neighbors' trees."

"Do you ask the neighbors if you can have them?"

"Sometimes."

Mom is looking a little stressed by now and Dad isn't looking. "You don't really shoot rats down there, do you?"

"Yup—big, fat ones."

"Do you shoot them dead?"

"No, they are too fat, but once in a while we whack them with our guns and kinda knock them silly, then we kick them and they don't bother us for a while."

"Oh, my God, there really are rats down there!"

"Yup."

"So, if you are fighting the rats down there, do you still have time to play war?"

"Yup."

"Who do you fight when you play war?"

"We fight Germans."

"Does your army have a name?"

"Yup. The Germans had a guy by the name of the Desert Fox. We really liked that name."

"So, you guys are also the Desert Fox?"

"No, the Desert Fox fought his battles in the desert and we fight our battles in the sewer, so we're the **Sewer Rats.**"

"Good Lord! Okay, let me get this straight. The German guy fights in the desert, so he is the Desert Fox; and you two fight in the sewer, so you are the **Sewer Rats?**

"Yup."

About that time, Dad started coughing and when we looked at him, he had both hands over his mouth. We sure hoped he wasn't choking! He must have taken too big of a bite, because we couldn't figure out why else he would be choking.

Mom leaned forward on the table and looked right at Dad and said, "Oh, Bob, this isn't funny …

"OUR BOYS ARE SEWER RATS!"

Chapter 13

Trouble in Kindergarten

"Quicker than a Sister"

Dateline: 1949 – Age 5

It was October, 1949 and I was in my third week of kindergarten at St. Lawrence. My teacher was a nun, and I liked her even though she was really old—maybe 50. She told us when we started the school year that she expected us all to be able to count to 100. That was no big deal; I could count to 100—did it many times at home.

Sister had a nice big, bead board with 10 rows of 10 brightly colored beads. She would call us up to the front of the room and have us count to 100 as she pushed a bead across the board with each number we counted. It didn't seem too hard and each kid did pretty well.

But, now it was my day and my turn. Sister said, "Okay, John Bruner, let's count to 100."

I walked up to her, stood straight, and began to count, "1, 2, 3, 4 … 29, 30, 31, 32 … 39, 40, 41, 42 …"

Holy cow; I drew a blank! What comes after 42?

Sister said, "Okay, let's start over."

I gathered myself and got off to a good start. "1, 2, 3, 4, 5 … 34, 35, 36, 37, 38, 39, 40, 41, 42."

Panic! It happened again. Why can't I get past 42?

Sister was irritated and I was scared. She said, "I'm going to give you one more chance, and if you don't do it this time you will have to stay after class and count to a hundred for the 2nd graders."

I was in the half-day morning kindergarten class and when the morning was over, the big 2nd graders came in and used our room for the afternoon. The 2nd graders were older and bigger, and I didn't like them. As a matter of fact, I hated them because I knew they would laugh at me. Sister said, "Okay, John, one last chance."

I fired off the first 35 with exceptional speed, but now it was 36 … 37 … 38 … 39 … 40 … 41 … 42 … Didn't have a clue what came after 42!

Sister said, "Go sit down. You will stay and count for the 2nd graders."

That was the worst moment of my life. I felt sick. I had to get out of there, and I did. As Sister turned her back and started to walk back to her desk, I bolted for the door. No more kindergarten for me—**I QUIT!** Sister saw me and said, "John William, you come back here!"

Now, just so you understand the lay of the land, our kindergarten class was in the basement of the school and so was the lunch room, so when you walked out of our room, you were in the lunch room.

Here I am sprinting through the lunch room, with Sister in close pursuit. I knew if I ran straight away she would catch me, so I took a sharp cut to the left and headed around some lunchroom tables. She chased me, but I could run in circles faster then she could. She stopped, leaned on the table across from me and said, "Now, don't move! I'm coming over there and we are going to walk back into the classroom together. ***Don't move!***"

I stood real still until she got about two steps from me—then blasted out of there! Here we go again, round and round those lunchroom tables. I liked to run. This was starting to be fun. I wondered if we were playing, but when I looked at her, she didn't look like she was playing. She stopped again. She didn't look too good. She was huffin' and puffin' and could hardly talk. I stopped and looked across the table at her. She said, "**Don't move!**"

She started walking towards me. "**Don't move!** If you do, I'll call your mom and dad!"

I was only five, but I'd heard that many times before.

I was trying to be a good little dude. I did as Sister told me. I didn't move until she reached out to grab me—then I shot out of there. She didn't chase me. She only hollered, "John William, you are in serious, serious trouble."

As I ran up the stairs and out the school, I hollered back, "So are you!" As I was running home, I couldn't wait to tell Mom how mean Sister was.

We only lived three blocks from school, so it didn't take me long to get home. As I ran up the driveway, I was surprised to see Mom standing on the front porch. I was so happy to see her, I threw my arms around her and said, "Mom, I hate kindergarten! Sister is mean, so I quit!"

I knew something was wrong. Mom wasn't hugging me back. She grabbed me very tightly by the arm and we walked all the way back to school. That whole trip back was a blur, but Mom was talking the entire way, and it wasn't happy talk.

When we got back, the kindergarteners were gone and those big 2nd graders were in my room. Mom handed me over to Sister then left. She didn't even say goodbye, good luck, or nothing. Boy, talk about going it alone— and I was only five.

There had to be 30 of those big 2nd graders in there and Sister said, "Children, today we are going to start our class with John Bruner. He is in kindergarten and he is going to count to 100 for us."

She grabbed her bead board, elevated it, and stood between the door and me. The escape route had been cut off. There were no windows, and I knew if I tried to wrestle Sister I'd go to Hell. So, I had to count and all those hated 2nd graders were glaring at me.

Sister said, "Here we go," and she pushed the first bead across.

I was frozen with fear but I said, "1, 2, 3, 4, 5 … (I was getting light-headed) … 6, 7, 8, 9, 10 … (my tongue felt stiff) … 11, 12, 13, 14, 15 … (my armpits started dripping) … 16, 17, 18, 19, 20 … (I was starting to get blurred vision) … 21, 22, 23, 24, 25 … (I couldn't move my arms) … 26, 27, 28, 29, 30 … (I was about to pee my pants) … 31, 32, 33, 34, 35 … (I couldn't breathe) … 36, 37, 38, 39, 40 … (I was beginning to lose consciousness) . … 41, 42 … (I was dying. I felt my little soul leaving my body. My whole life flashed before me.) Then, suddenly, I heard the number "43." Sister said it!

I opened my eyes and said, "44." She smiled. I'm not dead! "45, 46, 47, 48 … all the way to 100! All the 2nd graders clapped and cheered and Sister patted me on top of the head. I loved those 2nd graders, and Sister was the nicest teacher in the whole world!

Sister said, "Okay, John, you can go home now!"

I couldn't wait to get home and tell Mom how good I did. I was going to run all the way. As I opened the door to leave, there was Mom and there was Dad. At first I couldn't figure out why they were there. Then I did figure it out. They knew I was smart and they knew I could count to 100 and they just wanted to be there …

TO CONGRATULATE ME!

Me & Snap

Chapter 14

More Trouble in Kindergarten

"Kindergarten Dropout"

Dateline: 1950 – Age 4

Snap was one of the youngest kids in Carroll to ever go to kindergarten. Most kids had to be five or six to start kindergarten, but Snap was only four. Mom and Dad must have thought he was pretty smart. Why else would they send a 4-year-old off to school?

Unlike his big brother, he was doing well in kindergarten. He could count to 100, never ran away from Sister, and wasn't afraid of 2nd graders. As a matter of fact, he wasn't afraid of anybody! So, things were going good for ol' Snap 'until one cold, snowy December day.

He arrived at school in the morning, all bundled up in his hat, coat, snow pants, and boots. He took off his hat and coat and sat down on the floor to take his boots off. They were the "five buckle" kind of boots.

Because his hands were cold, he was having trouble unbuckling his boots. A couple of nuns standing close by were smiling at him. Snap noticed that and didn't like it. He thought they were making fun of him.

71

But he continued to work on those buckles and then he heard those two nuns giggling. He looked up at them and, sure enough, they *were* looking right at him and giggling!

That was it! He'd had enough. He buckled his boots back up, put on his hat and coat, walked right past those giggling sisters, and went home. End of story ...

SNAP DROPPED OUT OF KINDERGARTEN!

Chapter 15

Angel in the Boys' Room

"Touched Me"

Dateline: 1954 – Ages 10 & 9

The "Boys' Room" was a large bedroom in our house with three beds, two desks, three closets, three chests of drawers, a seven-foot ceiling, and lots of open space to do fun things. This is where we went to study, to sleep, to wrestle, to talk. We talked about friends and family and good teachers and bad teachers and good stuff and bad stuff and girls and ghosts and monsters and angels. This was our safe haven. We could visit about anything.

Snap and I spent some time visiting about angels, but neither one of us had ever seen one. We both wanted to see one, but we agreed we didn't want to run into one at night because that would be too scary.

We learned a lot about angels at our Catholic school, St. Lawrence, and the sisters told us we each had a Guardian Angel that protected us and guarded us and was there to help us when we needed it. That was good news, because we were both at a point in our lives when we could use all the help we could get!

In 1954, I was ten years old and in 5th Grade. My dad and mom helped me learn all the Mass prayers in Latin so I could be a server (altar boy). Every time I got to serve I felt very important and knew that I was doing something extra special for God. About every six weeks we would serve Mass every day for one full week. It would either be the 6:30 a.m. Mass all week or the 8:00 a.m. Mass all week. The 6:30 Mass was kinda early, but once I got up and got going, I liked it.

One week in November, I was serving 6:30 Mass. We only had one alarm clock in the whole house, and that was in Dad's and Mom's room, so when I had to get up to serve, one of them would come in and wake me up. They always said, "John, you are a hard sleeper!"

I think that meant I was hard to wake up and I guess I was, because when they would wake me up, they would shake me really hard. When I woke up, they were always there smiling and I was always happy to see them.

One night in the middle of this week, I was saying my usual night prayers beside my bed, and for no particular reason, my thoughts turned to my Guardian Angel. I wanted to know for sure that this angel was really there and really cared and really wanted to help me. So, I prayerfully issued this challenge, "If you are really here, wake me up in the morning at 6:00 before Mom and Dad come in to wake me up."

That was it. I didn't think that much more about it, climbed into bed, pulled up the covers and went right to sleep.

The next morning, either Mom or Dad was shaking me really hard and saying, "John it's time to wake up. Wake up!"

I sat up in bed, rubbed the sleep out of my eyes, and looked for Mom or Dad. They weren't there.

That was weird. I looked up at the large clock on our wall and the hour hand was straight down on "6" and the minute hand was straight up on "12."

Six o'clock—straight up and down. **Holy cow**! What just happened?

I jumped out of bed, raced into the bathroom, put some butch wax in my hair (flat-tops needed that stuff to stand up) and started brushing my teeth. While I was brushing my teeth Mom came in and said, "Thank God you're up; we forgot to set the alarm clock. How in the world did you wake up anyway?"

My mouth was full of toothbrush and toothpaste, but both times I tried to say, "Angel" it came out, "a-oh." Mom just smiled and said, "I'll have breakfast ready for you when you get home."

I was scared. I got dressed and ran as fast as I could the entire four blocks to church. As I was running, I was wondering if this angel was running beside me or just floating alongside of me. Either way, I was glad he was there.

Mass seemed to go fast and, when it was over, Father told me I did a good job. I ran all the way home and, while I was running, I kept looking over my shoulder. I guess I just wasn't used to having that angel around all the time. He made me a little nervous.

When I got home, Mom was in the kitchen and had French toast ready for me. She was up early every morning making us a good breakfast and helping us get ready for school. I know some mornings she was tired, and some mornings she didn't feel good, but she was always there giving us her special love and encouragement. I was the only kid in the kitchen at the time and Mom came over and sat down beside me and asked, "How did you wake up this morning?"

I was kinda embarrassed to tell her, because I didn't think she would believe me, so I answered her very, very softly, "Angel."

Mom looked stunned.

"Did you say Angel?"

"Yes."

"Did your Angel wake you up?"

"Yup." Then I told her about my prayer to my Guardian Angel.

About this time, mom reached over and put both of her hands on my right hand, looking at me in a real special way. Then she said, "How did your angel wake you up?"

"I was sleeping real hard like you and Dad always say. Then one of you was shaking me really hard and saying, "John, wake up. Wake up. Or something like that."

"But we forgot to set the alarm. We weren't shaking you. No one was shaking you, John. You were having a dream." Now Mom was patting my hand.

"It wasn't a dream, Mom. When I woke up and you guys weren't there, I looked at the clock and knew what had happened."

"Oh, I wish your father was here."

"I know it sounds crazy, Mom, but this morning at 6 o'clock there was …

"AN ANGEL IN THE BOYS' ROOM!"

Me & Snap

Chapter 16

Three Block Fist Fight

"Duel in the Street"

Dateline: 1955 – Ages 11 & 10

It was a hot, late summer afternoon. Snap and I were doing what we did almost every day—wrestling. We were in the front yard, the ground was hard, it was buggy, and we were hot, sweaty and tired. All those conditions caused us to get mad, mean, and stupid. I don't know who threw the first punch, but all of a sudden we were on our feet, standing toe-to-toe, flailing away at each other. Most of our fist fights would only last four or five minutes, no matter whom we were fighting. But this one was a beauty. It lasted twenty minutes and was fought from our front yard to St. Lawrence School—three blocks, or a little more than a quarter of a mile.

Snap was a couple of inches shorter than me, and his style was to always come in low and pound the body, then cut loose with solid uppercuts. My style was to fight backing up, throwing roundhouses to the head and neck. For an exhausting, bruising twenty minutes that's how this battle was fought.

We slugged it out from the front yard, into the street, onto Mrs. Schaefer's north lawn, back into the street, past the Stone's house, into Dr. Anneberg's back yard, then returned to the middle of the street. One block down, two to go. We stopped for a minute or so, caught our breath, called each other some bad names, and then started unloading rights and lefts and uppercuts and roundhouses.

Snap kept coming forward, pounding my midsection and busting my bottom lip wide open with uppercuts. I kept throwing punches to the side of his head and occasionally to his face. His ears were turning black and blue; his right eye was puffy. We fought onto Mr. Martin's front yard, back into the street, into a vacant lot and onto Mr. and Mrs. Frank's front yard. Two blocks down, one to go. We stopped and rested our battered bodies for a little bit.

Snap put his dukes up and said, "Let's go, you fathead."

I was hoping he'd say, "Let's go home," but his, "Let's go" was an invitation to keep on fighting.

So, I obliged him. Back into the street, past the Crouse house, onto the sidewalk, then back across the street. We had just pounded each other for three blocks, and were loading up for number four, when a loud car horn honked at us. Oh, my God! It was Dad and Mom. Dad jumped out of the car and said, "GET IN!"

We got in. Mom was so mad she didn't talk. That ride home seemed longer than the fight.

We were sent to the Boy's Room (our bedroom) to get clean clothes on, wash up and patch up in the bathroom and get ready for a "little trip." We dabbed blood and sweat off each other's face and knuckles and actually giggled softly about how much fun that three block fist fight was. We were warriors. We looked like warriors. We fought like warriors, and we weren't only proud of ourselves—we were proud of each other! It was a *Battle Royale*.

"Okay, boys—downstairs and get in the car!" Dad was in a real serious mood. We got in the car and hoped we weren't going to Boys Town. Mom finally spoke, "I called Fr. Peckus. He is waiting for you two in the confessional."

Oh, dear God, we liked Father Peckus, but when he got mad, he got mean. Confession to Father Peckus for a measly little three block fist fight? It didn't seem fair!

When we got out of the car, Mom and Dad drove away. We shuffled into church and there stood Father Peckus, by the confessional. He shot us a mean look and stepped into "*THE BOX*."

Who would go first? It was Snap, and I admired his courage. He entered "the box," and I could hear Father Peckus growling. A minute later Snap walked out, knelt down beside me and didn't look up.

My turn. I went in and started my required opening remarks. "Bless me Father, for I have sinned … ," but before I could say anymore, he asked, "What's the matter with you two? Are you stupid or something?"

I was about to say, "Yes," but then he told me if this ever happens again, he's going to use more than words. I knew he had a big wooden paddle and I'm sure that's what he was talking about. Then he said, "Now, you and your brother go home and say a rosary and say it together. Do you hear me?"

I said, "Yes, Father."

Then he said, "Go on, get out of here. Go home."

Still can't figure out why he was in such a bad mood.

We jogged out of church and when we got a block away we started laughing. I don't know why we started laughing. It must have been because we were "stupid." We were straight-faced by the time we got home and, when we walked in the house, Mom and Dad didn't say anything. I asked them if it was okay if we went to our fort in the jungle and Mom said, "Okay, but we are going to eat in a half hour."

We ran out into the jungle and climbed up into the second floor of our fort. We talked about saying the rosary and decided we'd better do it. We didn't have a rosary in the fort. We just had a little silver cross we kept there because we really did like Jesus and we knew that, most of the time, he liked us, too. So we decided to use our fingers and we were praying in a whisper when, all of a sudden, there was a knock on the roof of the fort.

It was Dad. He asked, "Are you boys in there?"

"Yes."

"Your mother and I have been thinking about you and we think it's important that you know something."

Snap said, "Okay."

Then Dad said, "Your Mom is here and she wants to say it."

We were both pretty nervous by now because that "Boys Town" thing kept going through our minds.

"Boys, your father and I want you to know that, even though sometimes you are bad and make us worry, we still love you very much. Having you two in our lives keeps us from ever having a dull day."

We weren't sure what she meant by that, but we did know that, for some reason, Mom and Dad were being nice. Then Mom said, "Did you hear what I said?"

We both said, "Yes."

"You are good boys and we want you to know we love you."

We said, "Okay."

Now Dad took his turn and said, "Are you boys okay in there?"

"Yes."

"What are you doing?"

This time we had to tell the whole truth, but before we did we had a few questions they had to answer first.

"If we tell you what we're doing, do you promise not to laugh?"

"Yes."

"Do you promise to believe us?"

"Of course, we will."

"Do you promise not to tell anyone?"

"Boys, we won't tell anyone. Now what are you doing in there that's such a big secret?"

"Okay, don't laugh. We're in here …

"PRAYING THE ROSARY!"

Chapter 17

Battleship **TITANIC**

"Lost at Sea"

Dateline: Summer 1957 – Ages 13 & 12

We hopped on our bikes and headed for Swan Lake with our Boy Scout hatchets and a couple bags of long nails, shoe laces, and leather strips. *Swan Pond,* as we called it, was a State Park three miles south of Carroll, with a 200-300 acre lake and lots of trees. We had a plan, and now it was time to do it.

We rode our bikes around to the south central part of the lake where there was a sandy beach and lots of trees. We parked them close to water and set about our business. We were going to build a raft and sail it across *Swan Pond* to a part of the lake that had never been explored. The northwest corner of Swan Lake, as legend had it, was inhabited by bandits, bad guys, escaped convicts, and wild animals. We really, really needed to go there because we really, really needed to discover the truth for ourselves.

We chopped down at least a dozen small trees, stripped the branches off, chopped the trunks into five - foot logs, nailed two levels together, and secured the nailed logs with shoe laces and leather strips. It was ready—our pride and joy. The raft was solid and going to take us to the North Shore. She was beautiful and we named her the *TITANIC*.

It was a hot, humid, dry, drought summer day so we took off our T-shirts, kicked off our tennis shoes, rolled up our jeans, and boarded the *TITANIC*. We each had a seven-foot-long pole that we carved out of a couple of tall skinny trees. These would serve as our oars and rudder, and we knew how to use them. We launched the *TITANIC* from the same sandy beach on which we built her. She floated and we were standing on her, headed towards the legendary North Shore.

It was exciting because this homemade ship was really floating and we were a couple of proud little dudes. We were out there two hundred yards, and then another two hundred yards, and we were going to land on the North Shore. Well, we weren't really going to "land." We were going to "look," then get out of there as fast as we could. Deep down, we were scared of what we were about to see.

Well, as luck would have it, we didn't get a chance to either "look" or "land." Water was pouring through the bottom of the *TITANIC*. It was above our ankles. It wasn't sinking—it was separating! It was floating apart. The nails, the shoe laces, the leather strips—they didn't hold. We were in the water and swimming as frantically as we could for the South Shore. We swam sixty or seventy yards and were out of gas in the middle of Swan Lake. Snap said, "John, can you help me? I'm going down."

I said, "I'll try," but as I put my arm around his shoulder, we both went down, feet first—down, down, down, to the muddy old bottom of Swan Pond.

But something happened on the way to our drowning. Our feet were on the bottom, but our heads were above the water. The drought was so bad and the lake was so low, we were actually touching. We could walk on the bottom! It was gooey mud and gooey silt, but we could walk and we could breath and we weren't dead. Praise God, we'd dodged another bullet!

It took us fifteen minutes to walk out of that hell hole and when we got out, we laid on that sandy beach for a half an hour. We were spent. Once our skinny little bodies recovered a measure of energy, we climbed on our bikes and peddled the three miles home. We were dirty and we were stinky and when Mom saw us she asked, "For gosh sakes, where have you boys been?"

We told her, "Swan Pond," and she asked us what we were doing there. We told her we built a raft and named it the *TITANIC*. Mom said, "You boys didn't cut down trees at Swan Lake?"

We told her we did and she informed us it was a crime to cut down trees in a state park. Heck, that was news to us. We'd been cutting trees down at *Swan Pond* for a long time.

Mom looked kinda worried, and then she asked why we named our raft the *TITANIC*. We told her it was the only name of a battleship that we knew, so we used it. Then she dropped a bomb and told us, "Boys, the *TITANIC* was not a battleship; it was a big passenger ship and it sunk to the bottom of the ocean on its maiden voyage."

We asked her what a "maiden voyage" was and she explained that it was the "first trip it made." Wow, just like our *TITANIC,* except ours didn't sink. It just floated all over the lake.

Mom asked what we did with the raft and we told her we put it in the water and rode around on it for awhile. Mom said, "Boys, that's a dangerous, old dirty lake. If that raft didn't hold you, you could have drowned! And, by the way, you guys don't know how to build a raft—did someone help you?"

Snap said, "No, we were the only ones at the lake."

Mom asked, "What did you do with this raft when you were done riding it?"

I said, "We rode it out to the middle of Swan Pond, it broke all apart and floated all over the lake. Me and Snap were drowning, but the lake is so low now we were able to touch the bottom, so we walked to shore."

Mom just stared at us and then said, "You two are muddy and stinky. Go to the basement shower."

We started down the basement steps and Mom said, "Boys, stop! I just have to know one thing and I want you to tell me the absolute truth. All that raft stuff really didn't happen, did it? …

"NO, MOM!"

Chapter 18

Dumb & Dumb "Or"

"Smack!"

Dateline: 1951 – Ages 7 & 6

In the fall of 1951, I was in 2nd grade, and somehow Snap made it back into and out of kindergarten and was doing quite well in the 1st grade. My 2nd grade teacher was not young, not happy, not healthy, not nice, and not very considerate of the fact that we kids were only seven years old and not very smart yet. Two weeks into the school year, she thought she knew who the smart ones were, who the average ones were, and who the dumb ones were. The smart kids, she put into the "Blue Group." The average kids were in the "Red Group," and the dumb ones were in the "Yellow Group." I was in the Red Group and I liked it there because there wasn't as much pressure to get all the answers right.

I'm not sure where this teacher came from, but she was slap-happy. Often, if we didn't know an answer or gave the wrong answer, she'd smack us with an open hand on the back of the head or the side of the face. She wasn't very big, but she could sure pack a wallop. I don't think a day ever passed in 2nd grade that she didn't pop a kid or two.

Anyway, one day it was my turn to read out loud to the class a couple of paragraphs from a story about *The Little Engine that Could*. I was moving along really well until I got to the part where the Little Engine was close to the top of the hill. If it had enough power, it would make it over the hill; **or**, if it didn't have enough power, it would roll backwards down the hill. Or something like that. Well, when I got to the "or" part of the story, I read it as "on," and immediately the teacher stopped me. She pointed to the word "or" and said, "What is that word?"

It looked like "on" to me so I said, "On." She said, "That word is not on, it's **or**. Now start from the beginning of the paragraph and get that word right."

Slap-Happy was beginning to make me nervous because she was standing right next to me when she was telling me "that word," and she was tapping me on the top of the head with her finger. I did as I was told and as I got that little engine close to the top—I stopped. There in front of me was "that word." I forgot what she told me, and it still looked like "on" to me. This teacher was losing patience with me. She asked, "What … is … that … word?"

I fell silent. Couldn't talk. Couldn't think. Could hardly see the word anymore. She started tapping me on the head again and said, "You tell me that word right now and I mean **RIGHT NOW**!"

I had to do something or she was going to tap a hole in my head, so I said it as I saw it, "**ON**!"

90

BAM!!!!!

She smacked me across the face, grabbed me by the ear, pulled me out of my desk, pushed my book into my chest and said, "Go across the hall to the 1st grade and ask your brother what this word is. He's smart."

Well, she didn't say I was dumb, but I was smart enough to know that I was dumb.

I walked over to the 1st grade room and knocked. Sister Donna came to the door and smiled, "What's the matter, John?"

All the kids loved Sister Donna because she loved all the kids and I always liked being around her because she always made me feel good. She was my 1st grade teacher, too. Anyway, I told her I needed to talk to Snap. She said, "Okay," and had Snap come out into the hall. Sister Donna went back into the classroom and Snap asked me what was going on. I told him I needed his help to learn a word. He asked me what word it was. I showed him "that word," he looked at it, and said, "I don't know. I've never seen that word before."

After he said that, he turned and walked back into his classroom. I just stood there. I was sad and I was scared. I had to do something. I thought about bolting out of there and heading home, but that didn't work very well when I was in kindergarten, so I decided not to try it again. I couldn't go back into my classroom if I didn't know "that word," so I was stuck standing outside the 1st grade room.

I was seven years old and my life was crashing in on me from all sides. I was crying a little bit and then all

91

at once Sister Donna was there. She leaned over and cupped my face in her warm hands and said, "What's the matter, John? What happened?"

I told her the story and then … then … she put her arms around me and hugged me. I didn't mean to make her sad, but I could tell she was crying. After a little bit, she rubbed my head and said, "Come with me, John. I can help you."

As we walked back into her 1st grade room, I saw her take out a little white hanky and wipe her eyes and nose. I guess she had a cold and I didn't care if I caught her cold because I really liked her.

Sister Donna told the 1st graders, "Class, we are going to learn a new word today and John Bruner is going to help us learn this word."

When she said that, it didn't scare me because she was smiling at me. She went up to the blackboard and wrote in big, big letters the word **FOR.** She looked at me and asked, "John, what is that word?"

I confidently said, "For."

She said, "That's right." Then she took the eraser and wiped off the **F**. "Now John, what's that new word when we take the F off?"

She made it easy; the answer was "or."

She said, "Very good! Class, John just helped you learn a new word."

When she said that all those little 1st graders started to cheer and clap. I looked around the room for Snap and when I saw him, he was smiling. Everything was okay now. I was ready to go back to my room. I said thank you to Sister Donna. She gave me another little hug and handed me my book, and I walked across the hall to a scary destiny!

When I stepped into the room I was told to sit at my desk, open my story book, and start reading the story from the beginning. Once again, I was cruising right along until I got that "little engine" close to the top of the hill. I slowed down … my teacher moved closer … my brain was gasping for oxygen … and … there it was … "that word" right in front of me … and … and I didn't know it. I kept trying to think of the word that Sister Donna had written on the blackboard. It was gone. Fear erased it. She was tapping me on the top of my head and telling me, "SAY THAT WORD. SAY THAT WORD."

I didn't know "that word," but I put my arms up beside my face and blurted out, "ON!"

BAM!!!

She smacked me, but it didn't hurt because I blocked it with my arms. She grabbed my ear, pulled me out of my desk, and pushed me to the back of the room. She plunked me down in a desk and said, "You are now in the Yellow Group!"

Well, that made it official. I was dumb. I really didn't feel that bad though because Snap didn't know "that word" either, so we were Dumb & Dumb—thanks to that word—"or." And, you know, at our age, six and seven, we didn't give a hoot.

That evening at the supper table, Dad was quizzing us about our school day. When he asked me how my day was I said, "Okay."

He asked, "Did you learn anything new?"

"Yes, I learned a new word."

"What is that new word? …

"I CAN'T REMEMBER!"

Chapter 19

Killed a Cow

"What's a Bazooka?"

Dateline: Summer 1950-1958 – Ages 6 to 13

We loved going to the creek. It was one of our favorite places to hang out when we weren't doing all that other stuff. The creek was east of our house, through the Jungle and about three city blocks across cornfields and pastureland. We'd take our BB guns, Boy Scout hatchets, some snackin' stuff and best friend—our dog, Fritz. Fritzy was a ten-pound, toy Manchester who went with us everywhere. We loved that little mutt!

We always had a lot of fun at the creek. There were frogs and turtles and water bugs and grasshoppers and snakes and horses and cows and even a donkey. One very mean-spirited donkey!

As we got about three hundred yards from the big pool part of the creek there was very tall, thick grass, that today is called switch grass. But we kids called it elephant grass and this elephant grass had a three-foot-wide path, all the way from start to finish. The path was the handiwork of that mean donkey. Now, when we were going to and from the creek, it was a lot easier for us to walk down that donkey trail than it was to push our way through that elephant grass, but whenever that donkey heard us coming, it would lay its ears back and come thundering down the path with bad intentions.

Well, the donkey never did get us because it wouldn't ever veer off that path into the elephant grass. So, when it got close, all we did was take a few steps back into the elephant grass and that old donkey would go roaring right past us. Now remember, we didn't start the bad feelings between us and that donkey. The donkey started it! So, occasionally when he would run past us, we would step out behind him and pepper his big fat butt with some well-aimed BB pellets. Boy, would he get mad and make some angry noises!

We used to like to hang around the deep part of the creek. We'd catch frogs and turtles and shoot water bugs and, for many years, unsuccessfully tried to kill a poisonous water moccasin. That ugly old snake sent us packin' many times. We would see him floating on a branch or a log and we'd open fire. He'd get alarmed and slither into the water in our direction and we'd head for the Jungle.

One day when Snap and I were out there shooting water bugs, Police Chief Bruening pulled up on the road right next to the creek and said, "Boys, come over here."

Oh, my God, it wasn't just the cops, it was the Chief. Dad told us he was a good man and ran a good police department, but we never thought the day would come that his job would have anything to do with us.

Well, that day did come and we weren't sure if we were going to poop our pants or head for the Jungle. Before either one of those things occurred he said, "You are not in trouble; I just want to talk to you."

We looked at each other, laid our BB guns down in the grass, and started walking toward this cop. He stopped us and said, "Bring your BB guns with you; that's what I want to talk to you about."

Oh man, we were scared. Someone probably reported us for accidentally shooting out their window, or accidentally shooting out a street light, or accidentally shooting a robin, or maybe even accidentally blasting that old donkey in the butt. Whatever, we figured he was tricking us and was going to haul us off to jail. When we got a few steps from this black and white police car he said, "Get in!"

He ordered both of us to get in the front seat and we did. We knew Mom and Dad were really going to be mad at us when we called to tell them we were in jail. Chief Bruening started his cop car and said, "Boys, did you know you were shooting your BB guns within the city limits?"

The city limits? We were at the creek. Downtown Carroll was a mile away so we said, "No."

Then he said, "You were shooting your BB guns on that side of the road and that's within city limits. That means you were breaking the law."

Snap immediately said, "If you don't put us in jail, we promise to never shoot our BB guns ever again."

Back then (we were only seven and eight), we'd say anything to stay out of jail.

"Boys, you are not going to jail. I'm just going to drive you around Carroll and show you the city limits so you know where you can and cannot shoot your guns."

Fair enough, but we didn't want anyone seeing us in the cop car so we slid down and peeked over the dash. That ride around Carroll lasted about a month, but when he dropped us off back at the creek he said, "Boys, that only took a half an hour, but I want you to remember what you learned today."

"We will."

He smiled and drove off. Me and Snap dodged another bullet!

One other day after school, we were at the creek messin' around, just Snap, Cy Farner and me. We were just doing our thing, blasting water bugs and talking about our teachers. As we were carrying on, we noticed a bunch of big, black cows moving toward us. We always liked those cows. We pretended they were buffaloes. I don't know what it was they were interested in that day, but they kept getting closer and closer. They were starting to scare us a little bit, so we picked up dirt clods and started throwing them. One of those big black cows got about six feet from us and someone launched a dirt clod that smacked it right between the eyes. That old cow's two front legs buckled and it crashed to the ground. **Oh, my God, we killed a cow!**

We ran all the way home, each guy denying he threw the fatal dirt clod. Before we went into the house we reminded each other of the "Code of Silence."

At supper that night Dad asked us how our day went. We said school was good and that we went to the creek.

He asked, "What did you do at the creek?"

We said, "Aw, just shot water bugs and messed around."

Then he said, "It's a good thing you guys have BB guns and not bazookas."

We asked him what a bazooka was and he said, "It's a big gun they used in World War II. It shot bullets so big it could …

"KILL A COW!"

("Oh Crap!")

Me & Snap

Chapter 20

Snap's Been Kidnapped

"I Know Where He Is!"

Dateline: March 15, 1950 – Age: Snap was 4

In Carroll, Iowa in 1950 there wasn't a lot of excitement. Oh, occasionally a car would smash a dog and all the kids would run out in the street to look at the guts and blood. And, once in awhile, some idiot would shoot out a street light and the neighbors would call the cops, but other than that, it was a peaceful, quiet little town. No murders, no kidnappings, no bar room brawls, no bank robberies, no nothing—until March 15, 1950, when the APB came across the police radio: *"Robert Brian Bruner, age 4, has been kidnapped."*

We were little guys, but we knew our way around the neighborhood. There was no way we could get lost within our playground, which was a six-square-block area. There were no bad people who lived there and there were no bad guys that would dare come there, but on this day, something goofy was going on. Snap was attending preschool at Mrs. Winniky's on this morning and for some reason I was home. Mrs. Winniky's was only three blocks from our house, so when the weather was okay, we'd walk there and walk home.

Well, the weather was good this day and at 11:15 a.m. preschool was out, so Snap headed for home. All the kids in the neighborhood were friends and Snap bumped into a couple of them on the way home. He and Butch Thomas built a few little mud forts in the street and then he pushed on to Ray Beck's house. Ray was five years old and for some reason was home alone for a little while. Ray had a neat basement in his house and we liked hanging out down there. It was like a cave. Like a fort. Anyway, Snap and Ray got to having fun and time just sorta slipped away.

Snap should have been home by 11:30 and it was noon. Mom had lunch ready and she was worried. She called Mrs. Winniky and was told Snap left with the rest of the kids at 11:15. Mom called the Kellys, the Martins, the Dolezals, the Farners, the Becks, the Wilsons, the Pudenzes, the Moens, the Stones, the Pringels, the Millers, the Schaefers, the Mormons, the Thomases, the Annebergs, and the Fitzpatricks. NO SNAP.

Mom called Dad who came rushing home. It was 12:15 p.m. and still no Snap. Mom called the nuns and Dad called the cops. By 12:30, we had cops and nuns in the house and neighbors all over the place. Mom was praying with the nuns and dad was talking to the cops. I couldn't understand what all the fuss was about. Snap was probably at Ray Beck's house. I told Mom I'd go get him and she said, "Oh, no you won't! You aren't leaving the yard. I don't want to lose you, too!"

I went up to Dad and told him and a couple of cops that Snap was at Ray Beck's house and he told me the police already checked that out and he wasn't there.

"If Snap sees the cops, he will hide from them. I know where he's hiding."

"John, we are going to let the police handle this. That is their job."

I still couldn't believe what a big deal everyone was making of this. It's now 1:00 and there must have been a hundred people standing around our front yard. Three or four of those little Ford black and white cop cars were parked out in front and a dozen nuns and priests were continuing to pray with Mom in the living room. Everyone was beginning to think that poor little Snap was a goner. Only a miracle could bring him back.

Now, Snap knew something wasn't quite right and when the cops showed up at Ray Beck's house, he hid behind a chair and Ray told the police, "Snap's not here. It's only me."

When the cops left, Ray and Snap went down to the basement to play. Ray's dad came home about 1:15 and gruffly told Snap, "Get home, everyone is looking for you!"

Snap slipped out the back door and headed home. He crouched low, staying behind trees and bushes, and actually got within thirty feet of our house, totally undetected, until Mom saw him and screamed, **"There he is!"**

With that loud proclamation, Snap stood up straight and stepped out from behind the bushes. And there, for one brief shining moment, stood Robert Brian Bruner—four-foot-two, red cowboy hat, black and brown cowboy boots, dusty old blue jeans and twin six-shooters, strapped low and ready to go.

The whole world took a deep, collective breath and with grateful eyes consumed the miracle of his presence, which was nothing less than ...

MAGNIFICENT!

Chapter 21

Cornfields & Graveyards

"Car Trouble"

Dateline: 1959 to 1961 – Ages 15 to 17

All of our lives, Snap and I loved sports and played them every day. We also enjoyed the sport of hunting. When we were in high school at Kuemper Catholic in Carroll, Iowa, we played football, basketball and ran track.

Most days, when practice was over, we'd grab our shotguns and head for the country. Mom was always good about letting us use her car, a 1939 light blue Plymouth, three-on-the-floor with running boards and a throttle on the dash. We knew very little about cars, but we could drive them. The running boards and the throttle gave us a huge advantage when it came to hunting jackrabbits.

Thousands and thousands of those beautiful jackrabbits inhabited the farm fields of Carroll County, and they were fun and profitable to hunt. We would drive Mom's car out into picked cornfields, put the front tires in the narrow corn rows, pull the throttle out to approximately 10-15 miles an hour, open both front car doors, roll the windows down, step out onto the running boards, lean through the car door windows with our shotguns, and travel up and down those cornfields, harvesting dozens of jackrabbits.

We filled the trunk with our bounty and then drove to the Unckelman Mink Farm, which was a mile south of Carroll on Highway 71, and sold them for 75-cents each. Heck, gas was only about 25-cents a gallon back then, and a box of bullets was only a dollar, so we were money ahead!

We never did tell Mom and Dad that we drove that car in the cornfields, but it was pretty obvious to all who saw that old Plymouth moving along the streets of Carroll that those corn stalks sticking out from underneath had to have come from someone's field. One evening at the supper table, Mom made it painfully clear to us that we "better not ever, ever drive that car into another cornfield."

She was embarrassed to drive her car around town with cornstalks "hanging out everywhere." She said we couldn't use the car again unless we promised, "no more cornfields."

We promised.

A couple days later, on a Saturday, we piled into Mom's car and headed for the country. The hunt was on. We drove out to the farm where our friends, Larry and Dean Feld, lived. We picked those guys up and drove into one of their cornfields. We weren't very honorable young men sometimes and this was one of those times.

We really believed we could get away with it if we just removed the cornstalks after the hunt.

Good plan. Bad boys.

We were right in the middle of this big, long cornfield when the car started to cough and sputter and sputter some more and belch out big puffs of black smoke. We got scared and bailed out of that old war wagon, running as fast and as far as we could before it blew up!

Well, it didn't blow up. It coughed up a little more black smoke and then just lay there. It growled a bit, then it got real quiet. It was dead. Real dead!

And, so were we.

Thank God the Feld boys' farm wasn't far away, so we walked there and they gave us a ride home. When we walked in the front door, Mom was there to greet us and asked, "How was hunting, boys?"

I said, "Not so good, Mom."

Then she looked out the door and said, "Where's my car?"

Snap said, "We had a little problem."

She then demanded, "Boys, where is my car?"

"Mom, it … ah … broke. And, it's in a cornfield … "

"A CORNFIELD!!! & $%^&+#*@!!!!"*

Somehow Mom and Dad found a way to forgive us, but it took about a month. Our family needed two vehicles, so Dad bought another car for Mom.

This one was a beauty—a 1953, two-tone brown, three-speed Plymouth with a radio that actually worked! They told us we could use it occasionally, but if we ever drove it in another cornfield we'd be grounded until we were fifty. We believed them, so this time we complied. That car never, ever went into a cornfield—ever. However, on occasion, it did go *into a cemetery*.

I don't recall who got the bright idea to do this, but once in awhile a bunch of us would go to the Carroll cemetery at night and play car tag. Yup, car tag (no one ever accused me and Snap and our buddies of being Rhodes Scholars)! The car that was "it" chased the other cars around the cemetery and when he caught one— rammed it—I mean, gently bumped the bumper—then that car was "it." We didn't do this very often, but the last time we did it we got in big, big trouble with the cops.

It was a cold winter night at about 11 o'clock, and six of us were playing car tag in the graveyard. We were having good, clean fun when a police cruiser pulled up to the cemetery entrance with red lights flashing. There was another exit, so we decided to run for it. We got about a hundred yards away from getting out of there when another cruiser with red lights flashing blocked our escape. Nowhere to go!

We were trapped. We were scared. And, we were in deep, deep trouble! We were ordered to, "Get out of your cars, and don't even *think* about running!"

Four cops converged on us with flashlights. They told us we were breaking the law and that we were "pretty stupid." We didn't know we were breaking the law, but we did know we were stupid.

Anyway, one of the cops there that night was a Top Cop. He was tough, so we feared and admired him at the same time. He did a lot to keep our town a safe place to live. No one ever did "give no lip" to this cop.

He took down our names, addresses, telephone numbers, and parents' names. Then he gave us a serious butt chewin' and told us to go home and wake up our parents and tell them what happened. He would personally be calling them in the morning. Then he said, "Now, get the hell out of this cemetery and don't ever, ever come back—unless you're dead!"

That one made us laugh a little bit. Then we thanked him and "got the hell out of there!"

When we got home, we went upstairs to Mom and Dad's bedroom and softly said, "Dad, can we talk to you?"

The light went on immediately and he said, "Is there a problem boys?"

"Kinda."

He told us to go down to the living room and he'd be there in a minute. When he got there, we told him everything. He didn't seem real mad, but seemed a little puzzled. So, to promote clarity, he conducted the following interrogation!

"So, you boys and some of your friends were driving around in the cemetery with your lights off, playing tag by banging into the other guy's car. Is that right?"

"Well, we really weren't banging that hard. We would just run into the other guy's bumper. And the guy that was "it" had to have his lights on. That was the rule."

"That was the rule?"

"Yes, sir."

"Did you know *your rules* had nothing to do with the fact that you were breaking the law?"

"Yes. I mean, we know it was stupid."

"Did you have beer in the car?"

"No, Dad. We don't drink."

"Did the police look for beer in your car?"

"Yes!"

"Did they find any?"

"Dad, we don't drink."

"So, they didn't find anything?"

"Well, they didn't find any beer, but they did find some cigars."

"Cigars? Do you boys smoke cigars?"

"Not really, Dad, but ... sometimes."

"Okay boys, up to bed, and don't tell your mother what happened. I'll tell her."

"Are we grounded?"

"Should you be?"

"YES!"

We went upstairs and Mom was there. She asked if we were okay, and we told her yes. We brushed our teeth, said a quick prayer by our bed, and climbed in. Mom came in and sprinkled Holy Water on us as she did every night, kissed our foreheads, and told us she loved us. We were eager to respond, "Love you too, Mom!"

As she left our room and was going into her bedroom, we heard this muffled exchange, "What did they do now, Bob?"

"Lorraine, you're not going to believe this one!"

...

"WANNA' BET?"

Me & Snap

Chapter 22

Busted

"Montezuma's Revenge"

Dateline: September, 1951 – Ages 7 & 6

We loved fruit. We ate it year round and feasted on it in the fall of the year. Our neighborhood was loaded with apple trees, pear trees, and even a beautiful, beautiful grapevine. It was all there for the pickin'— literally!

One warm September Friday evening, we decided to take our little red wagon and go on a "fruit raid." We told Mom and Dad we were just going to go down to the end of the block and that we'd be home soon. They said okay and I told Snap to hop in the wagon and I'd pull him for a ways so the folks wouldn't suspect anything.

We were only a block away from home and it was just about dark, so we had to work fast. Our first visit was to Mr. and Mrs. Martin's grapevines. We snatched four big bunches and moved onto seven or eight different apple trees. We had Dad's flashlight, so we actually climbed a couple of those trees and picked the best ones we could reach. We executed the raid quickly, quietly and efficiently. It went off without a hitch. We had 30-40 apples and those four bunches of grapes. We pulled our loaded little red wagon down an alley and through backyards until we reached the safety of our own yard.

We had a basketball hoop there and Dad hooked up some floodlights so we could shoot around at night. Well, guess what? As we were transporting our stolen merchandise across our backyard, the floodlights suddenly came on!

BUSTED!

Guess who was waiting there to greet us? Guess who almost pooped their pants? Dad asked where we got all the fruit and we told him, "The neighbors' trees."

"Did you ask the neighbors if you could have it?"

"We forgot."

Mom wondered what we were going to do with all that fruit and we told her we were going to eat most of it and give her some of the apples to make a pie. That didn't work because she still seemed really mad at us. She did say, however, "Boys, you eat so much fruit now, you have Montezuma's Revenge (diarrhea) most of the time. If you eat all of this, we'll have to put a *cork* in you!"

Mom made us laugh.

Then Dad said, "Boys, there is nothing funny about this. Tomorrow morning you are going to take all this fruit back and tell the neighbors you are sorry and you will never do it again. Now up to bed! Wait a minute, where is my flashlight?"

Even though we got busted big time we still slept pretty good. Mom fixed us a nice breakfast then sent us on our way. As we were pulling our wagon down the sidewalk, we noticed that Mom was still standing there. She probably wanted to be sure we weren't going to eat any of that fruit.

We went to Mr. and Mrs. Martin's house first and we didn't even have to knock because she was standing at the door. It was almost as if she knew we were coming. Mr. and Mrs. Martin were old people, but they were really nice—especially Mrs. Martin. We told Mrs. Martin, "We took some of your grapes last night and forgot to ask you and we are sorry. We brought all the grapes back and didn't eat any of them."

Mrs. Martin said, "Thank you for telling me this. My husband and I really like you boys and we want you to have these grapes and all the grapes you want. All you have to do is ask us whenever you want them."

We promised, thanked her, and then went to the other neighbors. Can you believe it? No one wanted their apples back. They all told us we could keep the apples and thanked us for coming to their house and telling them what we had done. Even though we were little guys, we were starting to get this whole thing figured out.

So, here we are, just about back home, pulling our little red wagon still full of all the fruit that we started out with and there was Mom. She hadn't moved. She was still standing there in the same place she was when we left to return the fruit. As we pulled our wagon up close to her, her arms were still folded and she said, "Did you talk to all the neighbors?"

"Yes."

"Why do you still have all the fruit?"

"They wanted us to keep it."

Then she said, "Boys, every time something good or bad happens in our lives, there is a lesson to be learned. What lesson did you learn today?"

Our answer was about as simple as we were, "We learned that if you steal stuff from someone and you tell them you were stealing their stuff, they tell you that they like you. And then they say …

"THANK YOU!"

Chapter 23

Books in the Britches

"Sorry, We Forgot"

Dateline: 1952 – Ages 8 & 7

"Boys, up to your room; I'll be up there shortly."

We were in trouble again, and it was our own fault. Mom asked us to stop wrestling in the living room and to "take it outside," but we kept rumbling around until we broke her favorite lamp. It was 5:30 p.m. and Dad was home. Mom was both sad and mad. And Dad wasn't just mad, he was *really, really* mad!

We ran upstairs to our room and prepared for a spanking. Snap came up with a great idea—books in the britches. There was a cartoon movie called, "The Little Rascals," where these three little guys got into trouble and put books in their britches so the spanking wouldn't hurt so much. Snap thought it might work, so we tried it.

Dad came in our room, closed the door and was not happy. He told us how upset Mom was and asked us why we were wrestling in the living room after she told us to go outside.

117

We knew what we did was stupid, but we continued to be stupid and said, "Sorry, Dad, we forgot."

"You forgot? Okay, you're going to get a spanking to help you not forget again."

Dad sat down on the end of the bed with his knees together and said, "Okay, who's first?"

Snap said, "I'll go."

He lay belly-down across Dad's knees and, just as Dad was about to administer a well-deserved spanking, he stopped. Tapping the bottom of Snap's britches with his index finger, he asked, "What's this?"

Snap answered, "A book."

"That's one of the oldest tricks in the book. Now, take it out."

Dad was smiling a little bit as Snap stood up, reached back and pulled out a thin, hardcover book and handed it to him. Dad looked at it and said, *Snow White and the Seven Dwarfs.* Good book, but there's nothing *Snow White* about you two. Okay Snap, let's get this over with."

Snap did as he was told and once again, before he began the spanking, Dad tapped on the back of his jeans. He tapped again, tried to hide a smile, and then told Snap to stand up. He asked if there was another book in his britches and Snap fessed up and said, "Yes."

Dad said, "Okay, hand it over." Snap reached back and pulled out another book. Dad examined it and said, *The Hardy Boys,* now there's a couple of *good* boys."

We didn't understand what he meant when he was talking about *Snow White,* but we did figure out the

118

point he was making with the *Hardy Boys*. He read us all the *Hardy Boys* books and those two boys solved a lot of mysteries and crimes in their hometown, so they were really good guys. We think he was comparing us to the *Hardy Boys.*

Dad didn't seem real mad anymore, but he asked Snap if he had more books in his britches and he said, "No, just a magazine."

"Give it to me."

Snap handed Dad the magazine. He looked at it, smiled broadly and said, "This is one of my *TIME Magazines*. What's it doing here?"

"It's an old one and we brought it up here just in case."

"Just in case what?"

"You know … "

"Then Dad mumbled something about, "Oh, Good Lord … "

Then he asked me, "Okay John, do you have books in your britches?"

I told him I only had one and it was a fat one because Snap put all the skinny ones in his britches. Dad put his hand out and said, "Let's see it."

I handed it to him and he read the title—*The Adventures of Tom Sawyer and Huckleberry Finn.* He started laughing really, really hard. As a matter of fact, he was laughing so hard he took his glasses off and wiped his eyes with his hanky. We didn't know what was so funny, but we laughed just because Dad was laughing.

When Dad finished laughing, he stood up, pointed the book at us and said, "PERFECT!"

Then he dropped the book on the bed and walked towards the door when Snap asked, "Aren't you going to give us a spankin'?"

He stopped, turned towards us and said, "I should. But I can't."

That didn't make any sense to us, but we were sure happy we dodged another bullet. At least, at the time, we thought we had. He then said, "Now, you boys stay in your room until we call you down for supper. No wrestling, no fighting, no noise—no nothing! Understand?"

"Yes, Dad."

It was boring. We wanted to wrestle, but didn't. We shoved each other around a little bit, but that was it. We talked about taking our BB guns out from under the bed, opening a window and blasting some sparrows and blackbirds. But, if Dad caught us he'd take our guns away, so we let that one go, too. So we just lay around, lit a few farts and talked about old people who smelled funny.

We were really getting hungry. It was 6:30, but Mom and Dad hadn't called us for supper yet. I went to the top of the stairs and yelled down, "Me and Snap are starving! When is supper?"

Dad appeared at the bottom of the stairs and said, "Boys, we've just finished supper and there's nothing left."

I pleaded with him and said, "But Dad, you said you and Mom would call us when it was time for supper, why didn't you call us?" …

"SORRY BOYS, WE FORGOT!"

Me & Snap

Chapter 24

Long-Shots

"Jail Time?"

Dateline: Fall, 1955 – Ages 11 & 10

Boys will be boys. And, even in the strict atmosphere of St. Lawrence Catholic Grade School, we did some idiotic things. One such thing was a game we played known as "Long-shots." This was a bathroom contest to see who could pee the farthest. The contestants would stand up as close as possible to the urinal, and then at someone's command, would take a single step back. Then another. Then another. And … the longest shot wins. It wasn't very complicated and most of the guys we ran with did it quite frequently.

Anyway, one day during the noon hour, four of us lined up for "Long-shots." It was me, Snap, Tony and Tank. We were all pretty even when, on our third step back, one of the nuns hollered in, "What are you boys doing? Get out here right now!"

Crap, the last guy in forgot to shut the door; and as Sister was walking by, she got a good look at "Long-shots." We were in deep, deep trouble and pretty embarrassed, too.

123

Sister escorted us to the Principal's office and told us to tell the Principal, Sister Superior, what we were doing. Sister Superior looked right at me and said, "Well, John, let's start with you."

I fumbled and stumbled around, red-faced, and finally blurted it out, and then said, "Sorry, Sister."

The other guys did the same. Then, there was dead silence for what seemed like a long, long time. Finally, Sister asked me what our telephone number was and she called Mom.

When Mom answered, Sister said, "Mrs. Bruner, this is Sister Superior at St. Lawrence. I have John and Snap in my office."

"Oh, Sister, what did they do now?"

"Mrs. Bruner, they were caught doing long-shots in the bathroom."

"I'm so sorry, Sister. Those boys know they should only do long-shots outside on the playground."

"Oh no, Mrs. Bruner! If they did these kinds of long-shots outside on the playground …

"THEY'D BE IN JAIL!"

Chapter 25

Hole in the Roof

"Snap Disappeared"

Dateline: 1955 – Ages 11 & 10

Risk, risk and more risk is what constituted the drum-beat to which our youthful lives marched. But on this hot Sunday afternoon in the late summer of 1955, that drum-beat almost fell silent.

For years, we spent a lot of time hanging around new houses that were being built. When the carpenters left at the end of the day, we'd explore the entire structure. We played Hide-and-Seek and Tag. Every part of the house could be used for these games, including the roof.

On this day, me and Snap and Cy Farner rode our bikes to a new house being built for Leo and Edna Fitzpatrick and their son, Brian. It was a beauty. They had just finished putting the roof on, so we had to properly initiate it with a game of Tag.

Snap was "it." Cy and I scampered in opposite directions in hopes that Snap would chase the other guy. When we played on other new roofs, the hole for the chimney was always very open and visible so, of course, we'd run around it.

The Fitzpatrick house had a hole for their chimney, too, but it was covered with black tar paper. Snap came charging over the top of the roof and disappeared down that chimney hole quicker than Santa Claus on Christmas Eve. We bailed off the roof and found Snap sitting on a large screen that covered the hole leading to the basement. Snap looked bad. I asked him if he was okay and he said, "No, I think I broke my back."

That just couldn't be true. We fell out of trees, tree houses and house roofs that were higher than this roof and never broke anything.

I pulled Snap's T-shirt up to look at his back. He had a deep, rather bloody screen imprint tattooed on his lower back. I told him we should go home and he said he couldn't ride his bike. I helped him off the screen, put him on the back of my bike, and rode him home. All the way, he kept his arms wrapped around my waist tight and laid his head on my back. I knew he was in terrible pain because his tears soaked the back of my shirt.

When we got home, my sister, Judy, was there and we put Snap on the couch in the family room and covered him with a blanket. No sooner had we done this than two angels appeared at our front door—Dr. Paul Cawley and his wife, Dorothy.

They were out for a Sunday drive and just stopped by to visit. The Cawleys were family. Dorothy was our first cousin. I told them about Snap and they rushed to his side. Just as Dr. Cawley was examining

Snap, two more angels showed up—Mom and Dad. They had been on a grocery run and just got home.

They rushed Snap to the hospital for x-rays. He didn't break his back, but it was severely bruised. He did, however, break his left arm. Dad came home and told us that Snap would have to spend the night in the hospital and that Mom was staying with him. I asked Dad if I could take my pillow and Snap's pillow and go spend the night with him. Dad said the hospital rules wouldn't allow that. So, I asked Dad if he would take Snap's pillow to him because I knew he would sleep better with it. Dad said he thought that was a great idea. So that night, my wounded little brother slept on his own pillow.

I left the light above my bed on all night. I was lonesome and I was worried and I was scared and I didn't want to take all of these things into the darkness of this night. I closed my eyes and I prayed—but I didn't sleep all night.

Snap came home the next day and looked pretty good. He smiled and told me to sign his cast. It was really good to have him home. Mom and Dad said they wanted to visit with us, so the four of us sat down in the living room. Mom said that everyone had heard about Snap's accident and that Mrs. Fitzpatrick had called with more angel news.

"One of the house builders," she explained on the phone, "got worrying about that open hole leading to the basement. So on his own time yesterday, he drove over to the house and built that heavy screen. He placed it over that basement hole an hour before Snap landed on that

127

screen! If he had not done that, Snap's fall (*and perhaps life*) would have ended on the cement floor of that basement."

It sure got quiet when Mom told us about the call. Then Dad leaned towards us and said, "Boys, you are both smart, but you are prone to do dumb things. You've got to stop doing these crazy, risky things. What if Snap died? Do you two understand death?"

We both said, "Yes."

Then, dad looked at Snap and said, "So, you *do* understand death?"

"Yes."

"Do you understand everything that death means?"

"Yes."

"Okay, then. What does death mean, Snap?"

"It means ...

"I WON'T HAVE TO GO TO SCHOOL ANYMORE!"

Chapter 26

Snakes in School

"And in the Boys' Room, Too"

Dateline: September 1955 – Ages 11 & 10

We were entertained by anything that walked, crawled, flew, swam, hopped or wiggled. One of our very favorites was snakes. There were hundreds and hundreds of garter snakes in our neighborhood, with the greatest concentration in Dr. Reese Anneberg's backyard. Dr. Anneberg lived one block west of us and, in his backyard, was a beautiful rock garden. In the rock garden, were many large, flat rocks and under those rocks lived snakes, snakes and more snakes.

We'd flip a couple of those rocks over and dozens of snakes would scurry in every direction. We'd grab the little ones and put them in our pockets and glass jars and the big ones we'd step on and then grab them by the back of the head. If we didn't do it just right with those big guys, they'd strike and bite us. That hurt like heck. Sometimes, they would even draw blood. That ended up being their last meal because we'd get mad and have to send them to snaky heaven.

It was the little buggers we enjoyed the most—the three to four inchers. They were fast and their bites didn't hurt. We would line them up and race them in the grass, the sidewalks, the streets, and sometimes even *in the house!*

Yes, we would take them in the house when Mom wasn't home and race them on the carpet on the living room floor. Boy, could they ever scoot on that carpet! One day when Mom was supposed to be gone, she caught us racing about six of those little guys on the living room carpet.

She got really, really mad at us and made us promise we would never, ever bring snakes into the living room again. We promised, and we never did bring them into the *living room* again.

We did, however, bring them up to the Boys' Room occasionally. Mom never caught us and we never did tell her, but we had some great races in our bedroom. One time, we lined up ten of those cute little snakes and turned them loose. They didn't go very straight. As a matter of fact, they went in every direction. We could only find five of them, so the other five just made a home somewhere in our bedroom. No big deal. We liked snakes, so we were good with it.

The snake thing really came to a head in September, 1955. Snap filled a sliding cigarette box with four of our three inch little friends and took them to school. After opening prayer, he got the attention of some of the girls and opened the box. The girls screamed! The boys cheered! And *Snake-Handler Snap* got kicked out of school.

When he got home, Mom was beside herself. She glared at the little guy and inquired, "What is the matter with you? You're nine years old and you just got kicked out of school!"

"Sorry, Mom."

"I don't care if you are sorry. Why in the world did you take snakes to school? I thought you promised to never bring snakes into the house."

"The school is not the house!"

"Yes, it is! A house is a school, a building, an office … any place inside!"

"Sorry!"

"No, you're not. Now, why did you take those snakes into school?"

"To scare the girls."

"To scare the girls? Well, it worked. You scared the girls, the boys, the teachers and everyone else in the school! Snakes are scary and should never be let loose in any building, in any room, at any time! How would you like it if there were snakes crawling around in the Boys' Room?"

"There are."

"What did you say?" …

"NOTHIN'!"

Me & Snap

Chapter 27

Ghost in the Attic

"The Door Just Opened!"

Dateline: 1955 – Ages 11 & 10

Our little brother, Barry, was born in 1950. He was a fine little fella and we loved him a lot; and to show our love, we gave him a lot of attention by teasing him a lot. There was never any harm intended. He was good-natured and believed almost everything we told him. When he was three, we nicknamed him "Toad" and he liked it. Everyone called him Toad, except Mom and Dad.

One of the ways we lovingly teased Toad was to scare him. Some of the scary stories we told him he'd want us to "prove it," so we'd just drop it. But there was one scary story we thought we'd have some fun with. It was Christmas time and we told Toad that *Marley's Ghost* lived in our attic. He just told us to, "Shut up!" and, "There's no such thing as ghosts, because Mom and Dad said so." We told him that not even Mom and Dad knew that *Marley's Ghost* lived in our attic, but me and Snap did because we went up there and we saw him.

Toad said we were liars and threatened to tell Mom and Dad we were trying to scare him. That's one thing about Toad—he was always squealing on us and getting us in trouble.

But this time, we told him we would show him *Marley's Ghost* if he promised not to tell Mom and Dad. As I recall, we offered him twenty-five cents, some candy, and a "nice" ghost.

He agreed!

It was about 8:00 in the evening and we took him into our sister Judy's room. There were two single beds in there. Snap got into one and Toad and I got into the other. There was a linen closet in the room, so me and Snap had opened it slightly, tied some string around the door handle, and ran the string up to the bed that Toad and I were in. Toad didn't see the string.

We told Toad that sometimes *Marley's Ghost* came down out of the attic into the house and that he always came down through that linen closet. Once again, he called us liars.

Snap began to pound on the wall and claim it was old, dead *Marley* roaming around in the attic looking for the door to come down into our room. Toad told us he was getting scared and that we should stop. We assured him that he was safe with us, but scared or not, *Marley* was on his way down.

Toad pulled the covers up to his neck and I gently pulled the string on the door. Snap said, "Here he comes!" and the door just opened.

Toad went ballistic.

He dove under the covers and screamed like a banshee. We knew Mom and Dad had to have heard that blood-curdling scream. We tried to calm him down by telling him it was a joke and that we were just teasing him. We showed him the string and offered him the candy and money, but he was freaking out and we knew what was going to hit the fan … **AND IT DID**!

Mom came storming into the room; it was very apparent she was on a mission. As soon as Toad saw her, he rushed into her arms. Boy, was she upset! We had never seen her that mad before. As a matter of fact, if she wasn't a pacifist, I'm sure she would have knocked us both ass-over-appetite!

She demanded to know what happened. Toad started telling her about *Marley's Ghost* and the door and all that stuff. We knew our goose was cooked. The infamous event closed with the following conversation:

"Look at your little brother—he's shaking. Did you think you were being funny by scaring the daylights out of him?"

"Yes."

"Do you realize now that this isn't funny? That it's harmful?"

"Yes."

"Do you realize you should tell Barry you're sorry?"

"Yes."

"Is that all you can do is stand there and say yes?"

"Yes."

135

"You two are really getting on my nerves. If either one of you say "yes" one more time I'm going to slap both of you. Do you hear me?"

"No." (A tiny little smile crossed her face.)

"Are you two sick or what?"

"No."

"Sometimes I think you both need professional help."

"What's professional help?"

"Professional help is when a different kind of doctor tries to fix what's wrong with different kinds of people—**LIKE YOU TWO!**"

"Now, go to bed and don't you ever, ever scare your little brother ever again! Understand?"

"No."

With that, she hugged Toad, took him out of the room, shot us another angry look, and slammed the door. Snap looked at me and said, "John, how do you feel?"

"I feel pretty good. How do you feel?"

Snap said, "I feel really good too ...

"WONDER WHY SHE THINKS WE'RE SICK?"

Chapter 28

WHACK!

"I Think She Loves Us"

Dateline: October 1957, Ages 12 & 13

It was a rainy October day after school. Me and Snap were up in the Boys' Room changing out of our school clothes into our jeans and sweatshirts.

Well, we started bumping and pushing each other and, before long, we were in a full blown wrestling match. We weren't mad. We were just enjoying throwing the other guy on the floor, on the bed, into the wall, and any other place we could get a commanding hold. It was fun! We were really rockin' and rollin' when Mom hollered, "Boys, knock it off! It sounds like the ceiling is going to come down. Now, get your jeans on and get your fannies outside."

"But, it's raining outside!"

"I don't care. Take your rough-housing outside. NOW!"

Snap and I put on our tennis shoes and fully intended to go outside, but as so frequently happened,

137

one guy bumped the other guy and away we went—wrestling from one end of the Boys' Room to the other.

It was fun, but stupid. And before we realized what we had done, there stood Mom looking down on us and holding something in her hand. We stopped wrestling, stood up and kinda smiled at Mom. She didn't smile back.

With that she asked, "Do you know what this is?"

"Part of the ceiling?"

"Yes. They call it ceiling tile and it's supposed to be on the ceiling—not in my hand. So, why isn't it on the ceiling?"

"Sorry, Mom. We probably knocked it down when we were wrestling."

"You aren't sorry now, but you are going to be sorry in just a minute."

With that she threw the ceiling tile on Snap's bed, left the room and returned twenty seconds later with one of Dad's belts.

"I'm sick and tired of you boys not minding me! Now, bend over and grab your ankles."

"Mom, what's with the belt? What's wrong with spankings?"

"You're too old and too big and spankings never worked anyway. Now bend over!"

Wouldn't you know? Snap had a plan. He said, "Okay, we will, but before we do, we have a confession to make—we broke the light above Toad's bed."

When Mom turned her head to look, Snap grabbed the belt right out of her hand. She looked shocked and mad and said, "Give me that belt!"

Snap fired back, "If I do, will you promise not to whack us really hard?"

Mom was really getting irritated, "Give me that belt!"

Snap persisted, "Not until you promise."

"Okay, I've had it! I'm calling your father."

We both responded simultaneously, "NO! NO! NO! Don't call Dad!"

With that, Snap put the belt back in Mom's hand and pleaded, "Please, Mom, don't call Dad. Please?! Look, we're ready."

And with that we stood there side-by-side and bent over and grabbed our ankles.

That worked. She grabbed the belt and said, "Now, let's get this over with."

But, before she could deliver the first blow, I said, "Mom, please don't whack us too hard. We are big boys now and we don't want you to see us cry."

Snap added, "Yeah, Mom, but if you do whack us hard, we want you to know that … we still love you."

That broke her! We could now hear serious laughter in her voice as she said, "Dear God, what am I going to do with these two?"

Snap answered with, "Pray for us?"

Mom responded, "That doesn't work either!"

Then she totally lost it. She couldn't stop laughing. After trying to regain her composure for a minute or so, she walked towards the door, dropped Dad's belt on brother Toad's bed, exited the room and with one last reminder that we were still in trouble— BANG!

She slammed the door.

We straightened up, smiled triumphantly at each other and then Snap said ...

"JOHN, I THINK SHE LOVES US!"

Chapter 29

Not Done Yet

"Back to the Jungle"

Most people don't read this part of the book—but you'd better read it (and **all** of it), or I'll send my *Guardian Angel* to wake you up in the middle of the night. Or, even worse, if *Marley's Ghost* is restless, he might just pay you an unexpected visit.

I want you to appreciate the following people who made this book a reality, so listen up! These are great people!

1. *My high school sweetheart and wife of 44 years, Connie, who inspired me with her laughter as she reviewed each chapter.*

2. *My daughters, Chrissy and Jenny, who were my cheerleaders with their emails, phone calls and hugs.*

3. *Our sons-in-law, Joel and Dan, and grandkids—Joel, Addie, Mason, Gabbi, Sophie, Johnny and Danny, all of*

whom "fire me up" with their special message to, "Finish the job!"

4. *Bill Sheridan, my very good friend and professional writer, who guided the process and cleaned up and smoothed out every sentence, paragraph and page and kept me laughing at every turn of every page.*

5. *Deb Albers, my administrative assistant of 20 years, who pieced together every word on every page and made thousands of corrections and only threatened to quit twelve times ... Great job, Deb!*

6. *My siblings, Toad, Lumpy, Buns and Mimi – they never once said I was "stupid" for doing this.*

7. *Cy Farner, Lorraine (Wiederin) Danner, Ralph Wiederin, and all the guys, gals and gangs in the neighborhood—thanks for the memories.*

8. *My mother and father-in-law, Bill and Rose Schreck, for the gifts of country living and their youngest of ten children, Connie Schreck Bruner.*

9. *Mom and Dad. I could feel their love and laughter as I wrote each chapter. One evening, when I was sitting in the kitchen writing Books in the Britches, I heard Dad laugh.* **It wasn't my imagination!**

10. *And finally, Snap. Was he a funny guy? Was he a fun guy? Was he my best buddy? Is he still alive and kickin'? Yes, to all of it. Do we still do some of this stuff? Of course we do! We were at the University of South Dakota not too long ago, having a few beers and a few Slim Jims at our favorite watering hole, Carey's. Do we ever go back to Tommy T's? Are you kidding? There's a huge, old bouncer and 5,000 old codgers waiting to kick our butts. We may be stupid, but we're not dumb and dumb "or!" Oh, and the Forts? Well, the old ones are long gone, but that girl I kissed in the chicken coop? She and I have been living in a fort since 1969 – FORT Dodge, Iowa!*

Listen, I've gotta go. Snap and I are headin' for the Jungle. If we get out of there alive, I'll tell you all about it!

John William Bruner

"Sewer Rats"